AN EXAM GUIDE TO
BRITISH SOCIAL AND ECONOMIC
HISTORY (1750–1950)

V. T. J. ARKELL & L. W. THATCHER

Oxford University Press 1983

Contents

The Publishers would like to thank the
Exam Boards who gave permission for the
inclusion of past examination questions.

0 19 913280 1

© Oxford University Press 1983

Oxford University Press, Walton Street, Oxford OX2 6DP
London Glasgow New York Toronto
Delhi Bombay Calcutta Madras Karachi
Nairobi Dar es Salaam Cape Town
Kuala Lumpur Singapore Hong Kong Tokyo
Melbourne Auckland
and associated companies in
Beirut Berlin Ibadan Mexico City Nicosia

Photoset by Rowland Phototypesetting Ltd
Bury St Edmunds, Suffolk
Printed and bound in Great Britain by
William Clowes (Beccles) Ltd, Beccles and London

Chapter 1 *Preparing for a History Examination*

Revision

If you are taking a history examination you should begin your revision early. Last minute swotting can so easily leave you confused with your memory crammed with disjointed pieces of information. Revision done over a longer period will be more thorough and give you time to make sure that you understand what you have learned. This is very important, because most questions which examiners set test the ability to think and write clearly as well as to remember factual information.

In preparing for a public examination, either the teacher or the candidates should study carefully both the published syllabus for their paper(s) and the questions that have been set during the previous three or four years by their board. If there has been no big change in the syllabus, then these past questions will provide the best guide to the topics that are examined most frequently and the form in which they are tested. From them you should discover how the time and effort devoted to preparing for them should be rewarded best. And if the examiners' reports on previous papers are available, they may also be very helpful.

Introduction to this Examination Guide

This book has been planned and written especially to help candidates taking British Social and Economic History at 'O' level. It is based on papers set in recent years by seven different examining boards. Its contents reflect directly those topics which have been examined most frequently by all seven boards. If therefore does not follow that all of these most popular subjects have been examined regularly by every board. Although this is true of the great majority, a few topics have been examined frequently by some boards and ignored by others.

Wise candidates will therefore check the frequency with which particular topics appear to be examined by their own board. At the same time, they would be well advised to check on the most popular time span for questions on some topics, like education, and also whether the questions apply to England, England and Wales, or Britain. Most Social and Economic papers claim to cover British history, but in practice you may find that your board regularly excludes Scotland from some topics and not others. (Because no paper covers the United Kingdom, no part of Ireland need be included.)

On whatever topic you write, the examiners will expect you to reveal accurate, detailed knowledge of the relevant historical facts. After selecting the topics which you are going to revise, you should make sure that your notes are clear and accurate and that you do understand what the main points are. Pages of notes which have been mainly copied from books are often of little help at this stage, and you should probably write them out again in a much shorter version, with the main points clearly set out and underlined. Then, you must also spend time checking that you have learned the names, dates, and other details. Candidates who cannot remember at least most of the main points for about fifteen to twenty different topics are unlikely to be thoroughly prepared.

Since this is an examination guide and not a course book, the factual information contained in each section is not enough on its own to pass 'O' level. However, the text does include what the authors consider to be the most important and helpful points for you at this stage in your preparation. Ideally, revision for an examination should not involve just learning familiar notes, but thinking about them as well. In this book, therefore, the factual information is presented within a narrative framework that stresses the main developments and indicates their significance. Inevitably the reader will meet in this text some new facts and ideas for the first time. A certain degree of novelty should prove refreshing and stimulating and so long as the overall interpretation remains familiar it should not cause confusion.

At times, with a few topics like agriculture and trade unions the interpretation may also appear new. This is because historical research during the last twenty years or so has undermined some traditional interpretations, and all the more commonly used course books have not yet caught up.

Weights, Measures, Money   In the text metric units are used only where they are appropriate. To aid the student the following approximate conversions are given:

1 acre	= 0.4 hectares	1 inch	= 2.54 centimetres
1 mile	= 1.6 kilometres	1 lb	= 0.45 kilogrammes
1 foot	= 0.3 metres	1 gallon	= 4.54 litres

Only contemporary money values are given in the text, but remember that there were 12 pence to the shilling and 20 shillings to the pound (£) until 1971.

Tackling the Examination Paper

Most boards expect their candidates to answer five questions in about 2½ hours. Normally, your first worry on receiving your examination paper will be to see if you have revised enough questions. However, when you do get your paper you should read the instructions carefully first, to check that you know how much time you have, how many questions you should answer and what restrictions, if any, have been placed upon your choice. As you read through the questions, your eye is bound to search out words and phrases that will tell you immediately what they are about. 'Trade union movement', 'suffragettes' or 'canal system' may be all that you need to know whether you can tackle particular questions or not. Then you will notice the dates and either be relieved or disappointed to learn, for instance, that the trade union question covers 1870 to 1914.

Once you have picked the five questions that you think you know best, you are still not ready to start writing. You should read each one several times to make sure that you have understood their meaning and implication.

Examiners rarely ask candidates to write down as much as they know about one topic. Normally, they set questions that are designed to test their understanding and ability to write clearly, as well as their knowledge. It is most unlikely that you will be asked to *Write all you know about the trade union movement between 1870 and 1914*. It could be *What were the main landmarks in the development of the trade union movement between 1870 and 1914?* On the other hand, it could be very different. To discover exactly what you are being asked to write, you will have to read the question again and think about it.

Why and in what ways was the trade union movement more powerful in 1914 than it had been in 1870? certainly is very different from describing the main landmarks in its development. You should also notice that the question is in two parts. As you read it once more this might become clearer if you thought of it as: *Explain why and describe how the trade union movement was more powerful in 1914 than it had been in 1870.* Clearly, this is no easy question. It will probably take you several minutes at least to think and plan what are the main points you should make and in what order. Since most boards allow candidates only about thirty minutes to select, plan and write an essay, you should not spend more than three or four minutes on the planning or otherwise you may run out of time for writing it.

Preparing for the Examination
With one exception, the 'O' level boards expect their candidates to write essays or continuous prose in answer to the great majority of their questions. It is therefore essential that long before you sit your examination you should start to practise reading and recognizing questions, planning your answers and writing them, so that you will do justice to yourself on the day. To help you, a number of essay plans are included and discussed towards the end of each chapter in this book. All the questions have been taken from recent 'O' level examination papers. In the later stages of your revision, you should concentrate just as much on preparing to answer these questions and writing practice answers as on learning factual information.

Writing Essays
History is a literary subject in which words will express your meaning. A good, clear, logical written style will therefore help you gain higher marks. This can only be improved with conscious practice. Whenever you use a word like 'they', for instance, make it clear to whom it refers, and avoid writing vague phrases like 'things improved'. Also, try to avoid unnecessarily long words, long sentences and long paragraphs. Each paragraph should have only one main point and each sentence should try to express one main idea. In your essays, each paragraph should follow on naturally from the previous one. This will happen much more frequently if you provide each essay with a logical plan or framework. And all really successful essays have an introduction that leads into, and a conclusion that rounds off, the main arguments of the essay. The best introductions are normally short and point clearly to the direction that the essay will take. Good conclusions may refer back to or complete the argument that was begun in the introduction. If your board says that extra credit will be given for sketches and diagrams, beware wasting time. Only include a drawing if you are sure that you can make your point more quickly and clearly with a picture rather than words.

Recognizing the Questions

At first sight, there appear to be no end to the variety of the wording and subject matter of questions set by the examiners, but in fact almost all their questions fall into one of eight categories. If you can learn to recognize them, it should help you to tackle them with more confidence.

Except for one 'O' level board, nearly three-quarters of the questions set usually come in one of the following four categories:

1 Descriptive essays
2 Explanatory essays
3 'Describe and explain' essays
4 Structured essays (in three or more parts).

With few exceptions, the other four categories appear much less often. These are:

5 Imaginary essays
6 Stimulus questions
7 Short notes
8 Multiple choice

In your revision, you should therefore normally concentrate on practising for the first four categories, but should not neglect those among the other four that are set by your board.

Categories 1 to 4

Some questions may ask you simply to: *Write an account of elementary education during the nineteenth century* or *Account for the increase of the British population between 1750 and 1850*. Although both of these contain the word 'account' they are actually asking two very different kinds of question. The first is asking candidates to describe the development of elementary education and the second to explain why the population increased. Similarly, many other questions will ask you either to *describe* what happened or to *explain* why events happened, why they were important or what were their consequences. Others will ask you to both *describe and explain* like the trade union question which we have met already.

Because questions can be worded in so many different ways, your main problem will often be to recognize what they are really asking you to do.

1 Descriptive essays Questions which begin with, for example, **What changes were made** *in the organization of poor relief by the Poor Law Amendment Act of 1834?* or **What were the most important landmarks** *in the history of trade unions between 1830 and 1880?* or **In what ways did** *the Labour government of 1945–50 develop the welfare state?*, are all asking for an account or description to be written. This might become clearer if the word 'describe' had been added to the start of these questions so that they became: *Describe what changes were made . . . , Describe what were the most important landmarks. . .*, or *Describe in what ways . . .*

But questions asking you to write an account or description can be worded in many other ways too. *How were housing and health improved in towns in the years between 1848 and 1900?* is another question asking you to 'describe how' but so even more confusingly is *Explain how road transport was improved before 1850.* This question contains a very misleading use of the word 'explain' because when it appears to ask you to explain how things happened, it is really asking you to say or describe how they happened. Therefore, this question would have been much clearer if it had been worded: *Describe how road transport was improved before 1850.*

Sometimes it appears almost as if the examiners get bored with setting questions with familiar wordings, and look for a format they have never used before. *Trace the progress of elementary education in England and Wales from 1833 to c.1900* would have been virtually the same if it had been set as: *Write an account of . . . , Describe the main landmarks in the history of . . . , What changes (or improvements or progress) were (or was) made in. . . ?, How did elementary education change. . . ?*, etc. All these questions in their different forms would have asked you to describe the main changes in elementary education and it is very important that you should learn to recognize them however they are worded.

2 Explanatory essays The other main kind of question is sometimes equally difficult to spot because of its various disguises. *Why did the cotton industry grow. . . ?* or *Why were there so many strikes. . . ?* are the easy ones to recognize. All questions including the word 'why' are clearly not asking us to describe what happened, but to analyse or explain why they happened or what were their consequences. Occasionally the phrase 'explain why' may be included in the question, as in, for example, *Explain why some industries declined and others expanded between 1918 and 1939*, but, more often, such questions are worded more simply: *Why did some industries decline. . . ?*

What were the causes of the depression. . . ? is another explanatory question, like *Account for the depression . . .* Both are asking you in different words to explain why the depression occurred.

Questions about results belong to this category too. *What were the chief results for nineteenth-century Britain of the development of railways?* is asking you to explain why the railways were important by showing what their consequences were. *What were the social and economic effects of the rise in the population. . . ?* and *What were the causes and results of . . . ?* are similar, and are asking you to explain or analyse. Inevitably, this will involve using your judgement and expressing your opinions.

Such questions are never easy to tackle because a narrative framework describing how the relevant events happened will not produce a satisfactory answer. And yet, as will be discussed in later chapters, they normally require the candidate to show, somehow at least, some detailed knowledge of the main events or developments.

3 'Describe and explain' essays It is mainly for this reason that questions which ask the candidate to explain or analyse are usually framed in two parts which include both analysis and description. You have met one already: *Why and in what ways was the trade union movement more powerful in 1914 than it had been in 1870?* This is clearly asking you to both explain why and describe how the trade union movement became more powerful.

Account for and describe the development and expansion of the iron industry between 1760 and 1830 and *Describe and explain the main developments in the British iron and steel industry between 1850 and 1914* are even more clearly questions which are asking you to both explain and describe. But such questions can be more heavily disguised. *Explain the most important changes that took place in the British iron industry between about 1760 and 1830. Why were changes necessary?* appears at first sight to be asking only for explanation. But, on reflection, once again the word 'explain' has been used very misleadingly in this question. It is almost impossible to explain the most important changes without describing them. Since the second part of this question is asking you to explain why the changes happened, the first part is asking why they were important, and in this case it would be much clearer if it had been worded like the previous one: *Describe and explain the most important changes. . . .*

These two-part questions which ask for both description and analysis are often some of the most difficult that you are likely to encounter. Both parts must be answered thoroughly. If you spend twenty-five minutes on the description and five on the explanation you will not produce a satisfactory answer. Because of the different approach in the two halves, you will have to think out your plan carefully in two parts to make sure that you tackle both properly.

4 Structured essays Some questions are divided into several parts like this one: *Describe the construction of the canal system in Great Britain between 1760 and 1815, and show how this helped the progress of the industrial revolution. When and why did the canals decline in importance?* To tackle this question satisfactorily, you should first notice that it is asked in four parts, and make sure that you answer all four. If they are asked in a logical order, as these four are, they will be a great help in making your plan. Here, you can follow the same order as in the question, and you also have clear guidance on what you should write about. Your main problems then become knowing what to say and deciding whether you should give equal time to all the parts. You should be able to describe when the canals declined much more quickly than how they were constructed, but you must still be careful not to spend so long on the first part of this question that you have to rush any of the last three sections.

Normally these structured essays, in three parts or more, contain both describe and explain sections, but not always.

Categories 5 and 6

5 Imaginary essays About half of the boards now include a few questions which ask candidates to use their imaginations. *Imagine you were one of the unemployed in a depressed area during the 1930s and write a description of your life during that time* is one such question. This is a difficult one to tackle because it gives no guidance as to what you should write about. Others are not so vague: *Imagine that it is 1835 and you are a Factory Inspector in the north of England. Describe a visit you have made to a cotton factory, commenting on the buildings, the work being done inside, the machinery, the working conditions, the factory owner and any other relevant matter* is a much clearer question. It leaves you with little doubt about what you are expected to describe. If only the question about the unemployed in the 1930s had suggested what you might comment on too, it would have been infinitely easier. As it is, it expects you to think out your own list like the one provided for the factory inspector.

One of the main dangers in tackling imaginary questions is the temptation to write too vaguely and generally. However, the examiners will expect as much appropriate detail in these essays as in the others, and you must make sure that you include it.

6 Stimulus questions A different form of question, which is set by only some boards, presents the candidates with maps, graphs, pictures or extracts from books or documents, and asks a series of questions about them. These stimulus questions are often very varied. Some can be answered simply from the information supplied and without any previous knowledge. Others expect you to have as much background information as you would need for an essay. But many of these questions can be deceptive because they rarely seem to refer directly to the stimulus material.

Practice on previous questions is the best way of preparing for these stimulus questions. You should also work regularly on documents, pictures, maps, graphs, conflicting text-books, or whatever it is that your board normally includes in its stimulus questions.

Categories 7 and 8

There are two kinds of questions which test little more than the candidate's ability to remember historical information. The papers set by all boards include either one or the other at least occasionally.

7 Short notes *Write about four of the following: the Speenhamland system; the New Lanark Mills; the Luddites; Prison reform before 1850; the Suffragettes; the Beveridge Report.* This is not like a structured essay where the different parts of the question are connected with each other. Here, each part is completely separate and you can also choose any four out of the six topics. In preparing to write such short notes, there will probably be no need to make a plan. The examiners will expect you to include as many of the main points as you can on each one, and they will mark you mainly according to the number of most important facts that you can include correctly. The order in which you answer them will not be important and since you will have only about seven minutes to write as much as you can about each one, you might even begin with the one you know least well.

8 Multiple choice At the moment there is only one 'O' level board which sets multiple choice questions. These are designed to test the candidate's knowledge by setting a question and requiring the candidate to select one answer from several suggested ones. Here is one example: *Who was James Watt's partner at the Soho Engineering Works in Birmingham? A Matthew Boulton; B William Murdoch; C John Roebuck; D Josiah Wedgwood.* The answer here is 'A'. But even if you know this, you might make a careless slip in the examination if you do not stop to think. William Murdoch was Watt's foreman at Soho and John Roebuck was his former partner in Scotland before Watt moved to Soho. If you hurry too much, you might just stupidly answer 'B' or 'C' even though you really know it is 'A'. Once you have answered the question set, you should move on quickly to the next and not waste time remembering other details about the one you have answered already.

The way to prepare successfully for such questions is fairly simple. You should learn a lot of the detailed knowledge which these questions are likely to test and you should also have plenty of practice at answering them.

Summary
When you come to take your examination remember to:
1 *Read your instructions and questions carefully.*
2 *Re-read the questions you decide to answer several times* to make sure of their meaning and that you have spotted how many different parts they contain.
3 *Plan each essay carefully* before you write it. You should spend about three or four minutes on drawing up each plan, which should have an introduction and conclusion and probably three to five main points in between.
4 *Write clearly and be specific* and not vague. Always try to illustrate your general statements with detailed examples.
5 *Watch the clock* from time to time so that you spread your time evenly between all the questions. It is always tempting to spend ten or fifteen minutes longer than you ought to on the first or second question and not leave yourself long enough to tackle the last one properly. If possible, finish the last question a few minutes before the end to give yourself time to read through what you have written to look for any obvious mistakes.
6 *Keep calm.* Whatever problems arise, you will cope with them best if you do not panic. The better organized you are, the more likely that you will do yourself justice in the examination.

Chapter 2 *Agriculture 1750–1914*

Agriculture was easily Britain's most important economic activity in the mid-eighteenth century. Many more people worked on the land than at any other occupation and the whole population was fed on food from British farms. The land also supplied the raw materials needed for making beer, woollen clothing, shoes, furniture, candles, soap, ships and many other articles.

In England only one-quarter of the farm land was owned by farmers. The rest was rented from landowners who usually maintained the farm buildings. The farms were small by modern standards. Many were about 30 or 40 acres, but those between 100 and 300 acres were most common. Labourers were usually hired for the year to work on the larger farms. The type of farming depended mainly on the soil and climate. Farms in the north and west concentrated more on pasture farming and were smaller. Those in the south and east tended to be more arable and larger.

People used to believe that between the middle of the eighteenth century and the early nineteenth century the traditional methods of medieval farming were abandoned in favour of a modern approach. Because they thought that the change was so swift and far-reaching they naturally called it the **agricultural revolution**. Their belief that it also depended directly on enclosures and the work of four particular pioneers stemmed directly from the writings of eighteenth century propagandists like Arthur Young. He greatly exaggerated the scope of these changes in a determined attempt to persuade his contemporaries to take them up.

During the last thirty years or more historians have shown that this is not what happened. Many of the changes began in the previous century and they continued in the nineteenth and twentieth centuries when some of the most revolutionary changes were introduced. Because farming practice usually differed according to soil, climate and location, few changes were introduced everywhere. Also there was usually quite a time-lag between the experiments of pioneers with a new development and the time when farmers took it up generally. For these reasons one cannot describe simply the farming changes in this period, and in some quarters the old-fashioned version of an agricultural revolution concentrated in the later eighteenth century still persists.

Enclosure

Most pastureland and over half the arable land in England and Wales was already enclosed by 1750. Most unenclosed arable land lay in a wide central belt that included the Midlands and stretched from north-east Yorkshire to Bristol and Dorset. There most farmers still sowed in scattered strips the same crops as their neighbours, and each year left fallow one of their three or four large open fields. After the harvest some villagers could graze their animals on the stubble.

Communal farming encouraged the lazy and inefficient to farm better. In the open fields some farmers also managed to exchange strips with their neighbours and consolidate their holdings. However for most farmers it was much easier to change their methods of farming when their parish's open fields were reorganized and enclosed with hedges.

Before 1750 most enclosures had been carried out by the agreement of all the owners of land involved. Enclosure by a special Act of Parliament had rarely been used because it was much more expensive. However it did prevent future disputes about what had been agreed, and it could be used to overrule the opposition of a small minority of the holders of land (say, one-fifth). After 1750 **parliamentary enclosure** became very common.

Parliamentary enclosure could take five years or more to complete. It was normally started by a parish's leading landowners, who might call a public meeting for those most likely to be affected. After 1774 notice of the intention to enclose had to be fixed on the parish's church door for three Sundays in August or September. Then a Bill containing details of the scheme was sent to Parliament. This was referred to a committee of the House of Commons which heard complaints. However few villagers could travel to Westminster and if the owners of at least 75 per cent of the land gave their consent, Parliament usually passed the Bill. Finally three to seven parliamentary Commissioners visited the parish to map the area, examine claims to the land, reallocate it and settle disputes about rights of way, claims to pasture-land or woods, etc.

In 1801 the **General Enclosure Act** was passed. It simplified the procedure by providing model clauses, but each parish still needed its own local Act. Only after 1836 was this unnecessary if two-thirds of the interests involved consented, but by then enclosure was almost over.

The Progress of Enclosure

Over 4,000 Enclosure Acts were passed between 1750 and 1850, with nearly three-quarters packed into two 20-year periods. In the 1760s and 1770s some 900 were passed mainly affecting the east Midlands and east Yorkshire. From the mid-1790s to 1815 some 2,000 Acts covered the whole central belt, with most in its eastern and western flanks. Except for parts of the south-east Midlands, only a scatter of individual parishes remained unenclosed by 1815 and most of these were enclosed by the middle of the nineteenth century.

These Acts covered over 6 million acres or about one quarter of the cultivated area of England. Over 4 million acres were in open fields. It is impossible to be more precise because some Acts were passed to confirm earlier enclosures, many covered only part of a parish without stating the acreage affected and others enclosed commons, wastes or meadows and not just open fields. Those in Yorkshire, Derbyshire, Lincolnshire and East Anglia were most concerned with commons and wastes.

The Effects of Enclosure

These were most obvious when a whole parish was enclosed. Then the village landscape was transformed with hedges, and compact farms and new farm buildings appeared in the fields away from the village. Such farms saved much time walking between strips.

When commons and wastes were enclosed and woods chopped down, many villagers found it difficult to graze their animals or gather fuel. Small plots allocated specially for the poor were usually little compensation. Many squatters and some copyholders, without proper legal documents for the land they occupied, lost their homes. The wealthier landowners, parsons and tithe-owners never lost out. Some also bought up the land of those who could not afford the high costs of enclosure.

Historians have argued much about how severely enclosure affected the lives of people in the villages. No longer do they blame enclosure for the surplus of labour and the poverty caused by the rapid growth of population, nor for depopulating the countryside. People did not move into the towns in very large numbers until after the main railways were built in the 1840s.

Enclosure gave farmers the chance to **alter their methods of farming** without bothering about others. In particular it made possible selective breeding. Some farmers continued to farm just as they had done before enclosure: at least for a time. Others abandoned corn-growing in favour of rearing animals and many more introduced new crop rotations which enabled them to do both more intensively. Such decisions usually depended on their type of soil, location and the movement of prices. When pasture farming replaced arable it could increase rural unemployment, but most enclosures created extra jobs with more intensive farming.

Farming Changes 1750–1840

The New Husbandry
Most of the changes which had been adopted widely by the mid-eighteenth century increased the fertility of various soils.

In **convertible husbandry** farmers grew corn and grass alternately for periods of about seven years. This improved substantially the heavier soils with the animals' dung and was adopted most widely in the Midlands. In the West Country, meadows near streams running off chalk hills were often made more fertile by being flooded during the winter.

On the lighter soils of East Anglia and elsewhere the **new crops** of turnips, clover and artificial grasses had been introduced from the Netherlands since the late sixteenth century. The farmers could then feed many more animals (mainly sheep) throughout the year. Their dung together with the nitrogen from the leguminous plants made the soil more fertile. Thin sandy soils were also improved by being dressed regularly with clay marl. Since light soils were cheaper to cultivate, many who farmed on them took the chance to grow grain by adopting the 'Norfolk' **four-course rotation** of turnips, barley, clover and wheat or some similar variation which supported mixed farming.

Upper Class Interest
By the time that Viscount Townshend (1674–1738) is reputed to have popularized the turnip in the 1730s it was already well established not just in Norfolk but also in most of south-eastern England. However he was one of the few great landowners in the early eighteenth century who took an active interest in agriculture. From then onwards landlords increasingly encouraged their tenants to adopt more agricultural improvements because they could eventually charge them higher rents.

During the second half of the eighteenth century concern with agriculture became fashionable among the upper classes. Even George III turned part of Windsor Park into a model farm. By forming agricultural societies and attending private agricultural shows, like the sheep shearings of Thomas Coke of Holkham (1754–1842), these landowners helped encourage and publicize some farming improvements. So did the Board of Agriculture, formed in 1793 with Arthur Young (1741–1820) as its secretary.

Prices 1750–1815

From the mid-eighteenth century Britain's population rose at an increasingly rapid rate and its towns expanded. This naturally increased the demand for food and led to rising prices for corn (corn prices had fallen or stagnated since 1650) and other agricultural produce. This greatly encouraged farmers to increase their output, especially during the wars with France (1793–1815), when there were several runs of bad harvests and extra grain could no longer be imported from Europe. By 1809–13 the prices of wheat had doubled compared with prices before the war, which helps to explain why parliamentary enclosure reached its peak in this period. More poor-quality land was also cultivated. Many wastes and common pastures were enclosed, marshes drained, woodlands cleared and the Cotswolds and wolds in Yorkshire and Lincolnshire developed.

Prices 1815–30s

The price of corn fell sharply after 1813 because of good harvests and the re-opening of the European ports. In 1815 Parliament passed a new Corn Law (revised in 1828 and abolished in 1846) to try to help the landowners and farmers by keeping out most foreign corn. However farm prices still fell in the 1820s and 1830s, especially wheat. This caused severe difficulties, in particular for farmers who had borrowed heavily, taken long leases or worked the least fertile land during the war. In these conditions many smaller, owner-occupiers sold up and other farmers were forced to become more efficient to survive. They managed to feed the continually growing population by developing further the earlier new husbandry and using other new methods.

Improved Livestock

The new fodder crops had enabled farmers to keep more animals for breeding. In the seventeenth century some had already begun to improve their sheep and cattle by importing rams and bulls from elsewhere. In the eighteenth century the number of successful livestock breeders had increased on the heavy soils in the Midlands.

Robert Bakewell (1725–95) began to experiment with the selective breeding of animals at Dishley in Leicestershire from about 1745. He pioneered a new method of inbreeding which involved mating animals from within his flocks and herds, and not from outside them. He selected his animals with great care, fed and housed them well and kept genealogical tables. And yet his attempts to breed sheep and cattle for meat had mixed success. His New Leicester sheep fattened quickly but their meat was very fat. His Longhorn cattle, which had already been improved by Webster of Canley near Coventry, also put on fat quickly and gave less milk. However, Bakewell was a skilful self-publicist who became so famous that he received many visitors from Europe and charged increasingly inflated prices for letting out his rams and bulls.

Bakewell's methods of selective breeding were more important than his breeds. Before he died other farmers had begun to apply them to other regional breeds. After 1780 Charles and Robert Colling of Ketton, near Darlington, developed a herd of Durham **Shorthorns**, which soon displaced the Longhorns because they were good for both beef and milk. Later, other breeds like Ayrshires, Devons and

Herefords were improved especially for milk or meat. These breeding methods affected the quality of animals on most farms only during the nineteenth century. By 1900 two-thirds of all cattle in Britain were Shorthorns.

New Implements

Although some pioneers had experimented with new machines and tools in the early eighteenth century, most farmers' implements remained crude and inefficient for several more generations. Only in the late eighteenth century did many farmers replace wooden **ploughs** with iron ones. Only in the north and east did they take up the more efficient Rotherham plough (patented 1730) with its curved mouldboard and lighter frame that needed fewer animals to pull it. Firms like Ransomes of Ipswich (founded 1789) made iron ploughshares in large numbers by the early nineteenth century. Harrows and rollers made of cast iron were also available.

Farmers on the light soils had also begun to use **seed-drills** and horse-drawn hoes. From 1701 both had been developed, but not invented, by **Jethro Tull** (1674–1741) on his farm, Mount Prosperous, near Hungerford in Berkshire and publicized in his book *Horse-Hoeing Husbandry* of 1733. Tull had argued, quite rightly, that seeds sown in rows at controlled depths gave better yields from less seed than broadcast sowing. If they were spaced widely, weeds could also be hoed out while they were growing. But his machines had been expensive and frequently broke down, and he had also argued against using manure and crop rotations. Even after James Cooke and others had improved seed-drills from the 1780s, most farmers still sowed seed broadcast until about the mid-nineteenth century.

Threshing corn by flail was one of the few jobs that underpaid labourers could do in the winter, so Andrew Meikle's improved threshing machine of 1786 did not catch on at once. It was used widely by 1830. By the 1850s steam-driven threshing machines had become common, although they could not clean and grade the grain in sacks until the 1860s.

Reaping machines were needed even more at harvest-time. The first major change saw the sickle replaced by the scythe for cutting corn. The Reverend Patrick Bell's early reaping-machine of 1826 was heavy and had to be pushed by two horses. Better reaping machines were developed in the USA and introduced to England in the 1850s by McCormick and others. After 1879, when Appleby invented a string binder that tied the corn automatically in sheaves, mechanical reapers came into more general use.

High Farming 1840s–70s

The period from around 1840 to 1875 is often referred to as the period of **'high farming'**. After the Corn Law was repealed in 1846 the price of wheat remained steady while increasing quantities were imported. By the 1870s the prices of barley and oats had risen by about 20 per cent and of meat and dairy produce by over a third. The mixed farmers were best placed to respond to these **shifts in prices**. Altogether the farmers still produced half the wheat and most meat and dairy produce required at home.

Farming prospered because the continued **growth of towns and population** increased the demand for food. **Rising living standards** enabled more people to have a more varied diet with less bread. Few farmers introduced new crops or very different rotations in this period, but many did grow more kale, swedes and mangolds as well as turnips for winter fodder. From the 1830s many fed their larger and improved herds on imported *oil-seed cake*, made from crushed linseed, etc., and from the 1850s on maize.

'Improving' Landlords

Some landlords spent large sums on erecting carefully-designed *farm buildings* for their farmers' more valuable animals. From the 1840s many also invested heavily in *draining* the wetter clay soils with relatively cheap cylindrical tile-pipes. These were laid regularly across the fields at over a metre deep. Successful drainage made the soil warmer in spring and easier to work, but many fields were drained inefficiently and few landowners made big profits even though the government gave many cheap loans after 1846. Altogether the landlords spent some £24 million in 1846–76 on draining and improving over 4 million acres of land.

Science

Huge quantities of *artificial fertilizers* were used to improve the soil. Bones were turned into superphosphates, basic slag obtained from blast furnaces, guano imported from Peru after 1840, nitrate from Chile after 1850, and some potash from Germany from the 1860s. Gradually some farmers became *more scientific* in their approach to farming. In 1840 a German scientist called Liebig had published a book showing how plants benefited from certain chemicals in the soil. It was widely read. In 1843 Sir John Lawes had established an agricultural research station at Rothamsted. And from the shows and journal of the Royal Agricultural Society (founded 1838) progressive farmers could learn more rapidly about these new developments.

Railways

These greatly influenced farming practices. By taking many farm labourers away from the countryside, they forced more farmers to adopt labour-saving machinery for sowing, reaping, threshing, etc. They also carried, rapidly, large quantities of farm produce to the towns, including perishable meat and milk, and brought back fertilizers, cattle food, machines, etc. Finally the railways combined with steamships to destroy the prosperity of British agriculture in the 1870s. Then the farmers looked back to this period as a Golden Age.

The Great Farming Depression 1870s–1914

Between 1873 and 1879 British farms suffered severely from a series of wet summers and *poor harvests*. At different times wheat caught mildew, cattle the foot and mouth disease, and sheep the liver-rot. The conditions were so bad that many farmers did not notice an even worse disaster. Foreign food was beginning to be imported in unprecedented quantities.

Grain

Reaping machines made possible the *extensive cultivation of the American prairies*, which had been opened up in the 1860s and 1870s by the railways. Steamships then carried the grain across the Atlantic increasingly cheaply. Between 1873 and 1884, for example, the cost of shipping wheat from Chicago to Liverpool fell by 10 shillings per quarter. British farmers could not grow grain as cheaply as on the prairies. As the **price of wheat per quarter fell** from 55 shillings in 1870–4 to 28 shillings by 1895–9, the quantity of imported grain rose from 1.5 million tons in 1870 to 3.5 million tons by 1900. Only one-fifth of the cereals consumed in Britain was produced at home by 1914.

Meat

In 1882 the first cargo of frozen meat reached England from New Zealand in a **steamship with refrigerated holds**. Within a few years ever-increasing quantities of frozen lamb from New Zealand, beef from Argentina and pork from the USA were coming to Britain as well as butter and cheese. By 1914 half the meat consumed in Britain came from abroad. Those who reared animals did not suffer so much as the corn-growers because the frozen meat was not of the best quality. Many dairy farmers concentrated on providing the towns with more liquid milk.

The Effects of the Depression

These varied from place to place. In general it hastened the swing from arable to pasture farming and from mixed farming to more specialization. The corn produc-ing areas of the south and east suffered most, with wheat production falling much more than oats and barley. By comparison the pasture farmers in the north and west remained relatively prosperous, at least until the 1880s. Stock breeders benefited from low grain prices and the demand for animal products was increased by rising real wages. Market gardening and fruit growing also developed near London and other towns. Many farmers only stayed in business by cutting their costs to a minimum and, where possible, employing fewer labourers. Prices recovered slowly between 1895 and 1914 but they did not reverse the trends of the previous years.

The government did not try to help British agriculture by restricting food imports like many other European countries because low food costs benefited the urban working class who had recently got the vote (1867 and 1884). Parliament contained the protests of the landed interest by appointing, in 1879 and 1894, two Royal Commissions which failed to produce any clear-cut recommendations. The measures passed were of comparatively minor importance. Several Agricultural Holdings Acts from 1875 gave tenant farmers greater security and compensation for improvements. The Small-holdings Act of 1892 helped some labourers become small farmers. Finally in 1910 many landowners started to sell off large quantities of land to their tenants who farmed it.

When war broke out in 1914 British agriculture was still generally depressed and it did not recover fully until the 1940s. Overall a new balance had been established. Britain would concentrate on making manufactured goods and the British people would get most of their food cheaply from abroad.

Statistics

Price of wheat per quarter
(in shillings)

1770s	47	*1850s*	54
1790s	58	*1870s*	51
1810s	95	*1890s*	28
1830s	57	*1910–14*	33

Agriculture in England and Wales

		1870	*1890*	*1914*
Cultivated area (million acres):	TOTAL	26	28	27
	pasture	11	15	16
	arable	15	13	11
	wheat	3.4	2.3	1.8
	barley	2.1	1.9	1.5
	oats	1.7	1.9	1.9
Livestock numbers: (millions)	sheep	21.6	19.9	17.3
	cattle	4.4	5.3	5.9
Milk production (million gallons)		500	700	900
Hired agricultural workers (millions)		1	0.8	0.67

Note: One acre is approximately 0.4 hectares.
Reliable agricultural figures exist before 1867 only for prices and foreign trade.

Guide to Questions

Agriculture is usually a popular topic with all boards. You should therefore probably prepare for questions on farming changes in both the eighteenth and nineteenth centuries as well as on enclosure.

Most questions set on farming changes in the eighteenth century are descriptive and 'describe and explain' essays. *In what ways was agriculture improved during the eighteenth century?* (London, 1980) differs only in the period covered from, for example, *In what ways were the years from 1760 to 1815 a period of agricultural change and development?* (JMB, 1980).

The following two 'describe and explain' questions show how similar they may be. *What was the 'Agricultural Revolution'? What advantages resulted from it?* (Welsh, 1979) and *In what ways did methods of farming change in the eighteenth and early nineteenth centuries, and with what results?* (JMB, 1977). In tackling such questions your two main problems will be deciding what to say and planning your essay. A detailed consideration of the first question should help give you ideas for tackling all of these questions.

Specimen Question 1

In what ways was agriculture improved during the eighteenth century? (London, 1980)

In your answer you must avoid a detailed explanation of why the agricultural revolution occurred because this question does not ask for it. Although they helped bring about changes, enclosures were not really an agricultural improvement in themselves. Therefore references to enclosures, prices, population growth etc.

should be kept to a minimum. You should also be careful not to unbalance your essay by including too much information on the lives of pioneers like Tull.

Suggested essay plan *Introduction* Farmers introduced changes mainly in response to price changes. Enclosures helped many adopt new methods, but they were not an improvement in themselves.

1 New husbandry Well established by mid-eighteenth century. Increased the fertility of soils and encouraged mixed farming with a) convertible husbandry on heavier soils and b) four-course rotation on lighter soils. Also marling and winter flooding of some meadows.

2 Improved livestock Selective breeding popularized by Bakewell—sheep and cattle—Longhorns and then Shorthorns of the Colling brothers.

3 New implements Iron ploughshares and also improved farm carts: many more with four wheels. Other developments like seed-drills, threshing machines and harrows were only pioneered in the eighteenth century by Tull, Meikle, etc. and not adopted generally until later.

Conclusion Agricultural revolution was spread over a longer period and did not depend on a few pioneers as was previously assumed. These changes enabled farmers to feed the growing population in the later eighteenth century and led to further developments in the nineteenth century.

Specimen Question 2
Questions on the eighteenth-century farming changes sometimes include the early nineteenth century (up to about 1830), but normally those on the nineteenth century alone do not begin before 1850. They come mainly in two different categories from the earlier period: explanatory and structured essays. The following two are typical and the second one will be discussed in detail: *Why has the period between 1850 and 1874 been called 'the Golden Age' of English farming?* (Southern, 1976)

> *To what extent, and for what reasons, can it be said that the period between 1850 and 1875 was one of prosperity and the period between 1875 and 1900 one of depression in agriculture?* (JMB, 1980).

Since the question is divided into four parts, they will virtually dictate the plan for this essay. It should probably be easier to discuss the reasons first. If you are well prepared to write a thorough answer on the 'Golden Age' alone, you may find it difficult to leave out enough of what you know on the first half to give yourself enough time to cover adequately the agricultural depression.

Suggested essay plan *Introduction* In mid-nineteenth century farming prosperity based on earlier developments and not undermined by repeal of Corn Laws (1846).

1 1850–75 Reasons for prosperity a) Rising prices of meat, dairy produce, barley and oats caused by rising demand: population and standard of living. b) Railways carried produce to towns and necessary supplies and equipment. c) Heavy capital investment and scientific developments.

2 1850–75 'High Farming' More intensive. Machinery, fertilizers, drainage, farm buildings, oilseed cake for cattle, etc.

3 1875–1900 Reasons for decline Falling prices, opening up of Prairies, bad harvests, refrigerated ships, no action by government.

4 1875–1900 Depression Corn growers suffered most, sheep farming too. Stock breeding and dairy farming had more mixed fortunes. Liquid milk prospered and also market gardening.

Conclusion   Picture of prosperity followed by depression broadly true: but it can be over-emphasized.

Specimen Question 3

The most popular questions on enclosure are structured and imaginary essays. Here are two representative examples, the second of which will be discussed in detail:

Explain the reasons for the extensive enclosure of open fields, commons and waste land in England between 1750 and 1850. Describe the procedure for carrying out an enclosure and the changes this made to the landscape and the life of the villagers. (Cambridge, 1979)

Assume that in a Midlands village in the late eighteenth century a proposal has been made that an application be submitted to Parliament to enclose the surrounding three open fields. Imagine yourself to be EACH of the following and indicate your likely reaction to this proposal.

> *a) The Lord of the Manor.*
>
> *b) A landless squatter living on the waste in a hut.*
>
> *c) A freeholder with land in each of the fields.*
>
> *d) The shepherd who tended all the village's sheep on the common land.*
>   (AEB, 1979)

Imaginary questions which give you a precise situation to imagine, like a village meeting, and ask you to write a speech or a letter or something definite are normally easier to tackle. It might help you here if you pretended that each person was at home explaining their views to their wives, for instance. Also because equal marks will be allocated to each section you must avoid the temptation of spending too long on any one of them like the Lord of the Manor.

In describing their reactions, you should include some personal details about each person as well as some relevant information about enclosure, village life or contemporary farming practices. You might also indicate what they have learned from friends or relatives in nearby villages.

The Lord of the Manor might have initiated the proposal for enclosure and be looking forward to making bigger profits and leaving a wealthier estate for his young eldest son to inherit.

The freeholder will be more concerned with discussing what new methods of farming he hopes to introduce. He will also wonder if all the upheaval will be worthwhile and if he will get a fair division of the land when it is redistributed.

The landless squatter has good cause for worry. No one of any importance will be bothered with him. Should he perhaps look for work in Birmingham straight away rather than voice his fears and opposition? Or should he approach the vicar for help and advice, especially since his wife has never really recovered from the birth of their fifth child?

The shepherd will certainly lose his job. However, if the farmers in this village follow those in some neighbouring ones and take up more intensive rearing of animals with selective breeding, he should not find it too difficult to get another job. But is he too old or is he prepared to change his ways?

Specimen Question 4

This next question sets multiple choice questions on stimulus material. It is part of a long one set by AEB in 1978. It will test your comprehension or intelligence at least as much as your historical ability. If you know the historical background well, it will help you to tackle the questions with more confidence. But you must still start by reading the stimulus material very carefully.

Enclosures: Stimulus Material A   *'With the enclosures a combination of evils fell upon the village: loss of the commons, loss of by-industries, pauperization by a demoralizing poor-law. Yet all this needs qualification. Loss of commons was a local not a general calamity, and enclosures were not invariably harmful to the labourer. If domestic spinning declined, there were places where other by-industries increased, notably straw-plaiting. The poor-rate in aid of wages was probably a contributing cause to the remarkable decline in the death-rate between 1780 and 1820. The same instinct to idealize the past which made weavers and frame-work knitters look back to a golden age, which had existed, if at all, only for short times and in exceptional cases, is seen in pictures of village life which are contradicted by actual investigation. Rural prosperity had been based on the labour of women and children. Low food prices had been based on the over-production of corn and on the poverty of the smaller farmer who sold the pigs, chickens and butter he could not afford to eat. The old poor-law had lain like a blight on the village. Pauper children, as they grew up, used to run away to be soldiers, thieves and beggars or sell themselves to the plantations to avoid the gaol and the gallows. The parish poor-house had been a place of horror, and was usually some ruinous cottage into which those of all ages, sick or well were crammed.'*

Dorothy George, *England in Transition*, Penguin.

Enclosures: Stimulus Material B

> *'Sweet Smiling village, loveliest of the lawn,*
> *Thy sports are fled, and all thy charms withdrawn;*
> *Amid thy bowers the tyrant's hand is seen,*
> *And desolation saddens all thy green:*
> *One only master grasps thy whole domain,*
> *And half a tillage stints thy smiling plain;*
> *No more thy glassy brook reflects the day,*
> *But, chok'd with sedges, works its weedy way;*
> *Along thy glades, a solitary guest,*
> *The hollow sounding bittern guards its nest;*
> *Amid thy desert walks the lapwing flies,*
> *And tires their echoes with unvaried cries.*
> *Sunk are thy bow'rs in shapeless ruin all,*
> *And the long grass o'ertops the mouldering wall;*
> *And trembling, shrinking from the spoiler's hand*
> *Far, far away the children leave the land.*
> *Ill fares the land, to hastening ills a prey,*
> *Where wealth accumulates and men decay:*
> *Princes and Lords may flourish or may fade:*
> *A breath can make them, as a breath has made;*
> *But a bold peasantry, their country's pride,*
> *Where once destroyed, can never be supplied.'*

Oliver Goldsmith, *The Deserted Village*.

Questions (A selection from the original twenty questions set.)

1 *Which of the following does Stimulus Material A suggest were characteristics of village life before enclosure?*
  1 Prosperity for the domestic weaver
  2 Real prosperity was rare
  3 Harsh treatment of paupers
  4 Plenty of food for the small farmer to eat
  A. 1 & 2 only; B. 2 & 3 only; C. 1 & 4 only; D. 3 & 4 only.

2 *Stimulus Material A modifies the picture of evils following enclosure by showing that*
  1 new by-industries sometimes replaced domestic spinning
  2 women and children no longer had to labour in the village
  3 the prices of foodstuff went down
  4 the poor-rate in aid of wages probably saved many from starvation
  A. 1 & 2 only; B. 2 & 3 only; C. 1 & 4 only; D. 3 & 4 only.

3 *Stimulus Material B suggests that the village had become depopulated because*
  A the occupants were terrified of the Lord of the Manor
  B following enclosure the village land was possessed by one owner
  C much of the land had become unsuitable for cultivation
  D there were higher wages in the new factories

4 *In writing 'The Deserted Village' Goldsmith, in Stimulus Material B, reveals*
  1 historical accuracy
  2 poetic licence
  3 nostalgia
  4 insincerity
  A. 1 & 2 only; B. 2 & 3 only; C. 1 & 4 only; D. 3 & 4 only.

5 *Which pair of adjectives best describes the respective outlooks of the writers of Stimulus Material A and B?*
  A Realistic—hopeful
  B Pessimistic—optimistic
  C Objective—subjective
  D Irresponsible—bitter

6 *Which of the following does the poet in Stimulus Material B believe to be essential to the prosperity of the countryside?*
  A. Men; B. Money; C. Sports; D. Wild Life.

7 *Upon which of the following matters does Stimulus Material A question Stimulus Material B's picture of village life before enclosures?*
  1 The position of the small farmer
  2 The provision made for the poor
  3 The availability of common lands
  4 The neglect of farming
  A. 1 & 2 only; B. 2 & 3 only; C. 1 & 4 only; D. 3 & 4 only.

8 *Which of the following is NOT an element in the poet's regret for the changes brought about by enclosure, as described in Stimulus Material B?*
  A The decay of the rural environment
  B Social change
  C The underlying materialism
  D The loss of wealth

This is not an easy question. You will tackle ones like this best if you concentrate on each part separately and stick very firmly to the question that is being asked. No one wants to know, for instance, your opinions on the passage from Dorothy George's book which was published originally in 1931. You must simply work out the answer to each specific question. For the answers see page 21.

Specimen Question 5

You may occasionally encounter 'short notes' questions on agriculture, like the following:

State the main facts about FOUR of the following, and show their importance in the development of British agriculture:

a) the Four-course Rotation;   b) Robert Bakewell;

c) Arthur Young;   d) Coke of Holkham;   e) the Royal Agricultural Society;

f) tile drainage;   g) Rothamsted.   (Oxford, 1977)

In your answer to a question like this you should always try to divide your time equally between the four parts you choose to tackle. Also make sure that you say why each topic is important as well as stating briefly the main facts about it. The text of the main part of this chapter includes enough on the *Four-course rotation* and *Bakewell* for you to be able to do a) and b). The following paragraphs contain extra information on c) and d).

c) Arthur Young (1741–1820) was educated in Suffolk. As a young man he was not a successful farmer. He then became a famous agricultural journalist, touring England, Ireland, France and Italy and publishing over thirty books between 1767 and 1815. From 1784 to 1809 he edited *Annals of Agriculture* and in 1793 he became the first secretary of the Board of Agriculture. Young consistently attacked the open-field system as inefficient and supported enclosures, large farms and the new farming methods. Much that he wrote was biased, overstated, inaccurate or contradictory, but he was still a successful journalist. He helped inflate the reputations of some agricultural pioneers and popularize among landowners some farming changes, but he had little direct influence on the adoption of the improved methods by farmers.

d) Coke of Holkham   Thomas Coke (1754–1842) became the largest landowner in Norfolk when he inherited the Holkham estates of 30,000 acres in 1776. From his rents he had an income of £12,300 a year. By 1816 they had risen to £25,700: partly because of inflation. Coke used long leases to encourage his tenants to improve their land and to adopt more efficient four- to six-year crop rotations. From 1778 to 1821 his annual sheep shearings were attended by many visitors who came to admire his Southdown sheep and Devon cattle and to hear about new crops and farm implements. Coke was a keen and successful landowner and farmer and popularizer of improved agriculture, but not an innovator.

Coke was an active politician, an MP for 51 years, supported Fox against Pitt and became Earl of Leicester in 1837. His wealth, hospitality and influence led to his agricultural reputation growing out of all proportion to reality. Eventually it was claimed that his estates were barren when he took them over, that his rents rose from £2,200 to £20,000 a year and that he was one of the four main pioneers of the 'agricultural revolution'. In his later years Coke did nothing to correct these misleading stories. They were useful for silencing his political opponents.

It is difficult to understand why questions like this continue to be asked about Coke. In 1955 R. A. C. Parker demonstrated beyond any doubt how inflated his reputation had become. Similarly examiners may also set a question on 'turnip' Townshend, whose earlier reputation as an agricultural pioneer was even less justified than Coke's. It stemmed from the writings of eighteenth-century propagandists like Arthur Young.

Viscount Townshend (1674–1738) was educated at Eton and Cambridge University. He was an active politician, becoming Secretary of State in 1714–16 and 1721–30. He then resigned after failing to persuade his brother-in-law, Robert Walpole, who was Prime Minister, to declare war against Austria and Prussia in support of Spain. Townshend then retired to his family estates at Rainham, near King's Lynn in Norfolk, which he had inherited in 1687. There he is reputed to have devoted himself to agricultural improvement, growing turnips and clover and developing the 'Norfolk' four-course rotation, and to improving the land with marl, manure and drainage. But in practice Townshend only took an interest in, and helped to popularize methods which had been well established in his part of Norfolk since the mid-seventeenth century.

Answers

Specimen Question 4
1 B; 2 C; 3 B; 4 B; 5 C; 6 A; 7 A; 8 D.

Chapter 3 *Industry*

Many different industries flourished in England in the mid-eighteenth century, producing a wide range of goods made from wood, iron, glass, pottery, leather, silk, wool, etc. Contemporaries like Defoe were very impressed by the variety and quality of their products. By our standards, however, the range was very limited and the equipment which made them very simple. Also, in most industries people either worked at home or in very small groups, and as often in the countryside as in towns.

The introduction of large-scale industry with goods being mass produced in factories by power-driven machines was a real revolution. It required efficient steam-engines and large quantities of good quality iron as well as money and organization. Although most of the developments which constituted this **industrial revolution** had started in Britain by the later eighteenth century, they did not emerge fully until the nineteenth century. Then they transformed the making of cotton first before spreading to many other industries.

This chapter starts with the crucial development of steam power. Then it describes the transformation of cotton and the development of the factory system and concludes with the expansion of iron and steel making.

Steam Power to 1830s

The steam-engine was the single most important invention which triggered off the rapid industrial development of the nineteenth century. All machines need power and in the early eighteenth century most were worked by humans or animals, like spinning wheels and horse-gins. Wind-mills and water-mills all over the country ground corn into flour. Some wind-mills also pumped water and, as the century progressed, more and more water-wheels were used to operate textile machines and hammers and bellows for iron making. Large overshot wheels were the most powerful (but even they rarely generated more than 12 horsepower).

Atmospheric Engine
The principles of steam power had been known to the ancient Greeks, but not until the end of the seventeenth century was steam harnessed effectively to a machine: for pumping flood water out of Cornish copper mines. Thomas Savery's 'engine to raise water by fire' (patented 1698) was dangerous and could raise small quantities barely ten metres at a time.

From 1706 onwards Savery's engine was developed by **Thomas Newcomen** (1663–1729) a Dartmouth blacksmith. By 1712 an improved Newcomen engine was pumping water from a coal mine at Dudley in Staffordshire. It could raise about 50 litres nearly 50 metres ten times every minute. Newcomen's was not a complete steam-engine since steam pressure pushed up the piston, but atmospheric pressure brought it down. Because the cylinder was alternately heated and cooled for each stroke of the piston, the engine consumed a lot of coal. This did not matter when it worked in coal mines, but where there was no coal, as in Cornwall, it was very expensive.

However, after Newcomen's patent expired in 1733, similar engines were widely used. Some pumped extra water onto water-wheels or into towns, but most pumped water out of mines. By 1775 sixty had been installed in Cornwall and over 100 in the north-eastern coalfield. Some were also exported to France and other European countries.

James Watt (1736–1819)

This engine was vastly improved by Watt, who was born the son of a master carpenter and shipwright at Greenock in Scotland. After serving a one-year apprenticeship as a mathematical instrument maker in London, he was eventually employed by Glasgow University in 1757 to make instruments.

In 1763 Watt was asked to repair the university's demonstration model of a Newcomen engine. He was soon struck by the inefficiency of continually heating and cooling the cylinder and experimented with ways of improving it. By 1765 he had developed a **separate condenser** cylinder where the steam was cooled. The main cylinder therefore remained hot and coal consumption was cut by half.

Professor Joseph Black, who taught chemistry, introduced Watt to **John Roebuck** who owned the Carron ironworks and became Watt's partner to produce full-sized engines. They took out a patent in 1769 but failed because Roebuck's engineers could not make the parts accurately enough. By 1773 Roebuck had gone bankrupt and Watt, who had given up his job at Glasgow University, had taken up surveying the Caledonian Canal to earn his living.

Boulton and Watt

Watt was rescued by a Birmingham industrialist, Matthew Boulton (1728–1809), who was owed £1,200 by Roebuck. With the help of two wealthy wives, Boulton had greatly expanded his father's business. By 1765 he had built a huge factory at **Soho**, north of Birmingham, where he employed nearly 700 skilled craftsmen to make high quality small metal articles like buttons, buckles, clocks and snuff-boxes. The nearby Hockley Brook could not keep his machinery running throughout the year and so Boulton was looking for an efficient pumping engine to draw extra water to drive his water-wheel. He therefore let Roebuck off his debt in return for his two-third share of the partnership with Watt.

In 1774 Watt moved to Birmingham with an engine which he soon rebuilt satisfactorily with the help of Boulton's skilled workers and John Wilkinson, a Shropshire ironmaster who had just invented a new lathe for boring cannon more accurately than ever before. In 1775 Boulton and Watt's patent was renewed for twenty-five years. At first they made only steam pumps, but with the help of the Soho works foreman, **William Murdock**, Watt transformed his pump during the 1780s with four major inventions.

1 In 1781 they developed the **sun and planet** gear which turned the piston's up and down movement into rotary motion for turning machines. A crankshaft was more efficient, but it had just been patented by James Pickard. Boulton and Watt therefore used the more complicated sun and planet system at least until after Pickard's patent expired in 1794.

2 In 1782 Watt patented **double-acting motion**, in which steam drove the piston

downwards as well as up. It was now completely a steam-engine: with increased power and reduced coal consumption.

3　In 1784 *parallel motion* followed. Watt replaced the chain that connected the piston to the beam with a rod and ensured that both rods from the ends of the beam worked in parallel and so more efficiently.

4　In 1788 the *governor* further smoothed out the running of the engine by reducing variations of speed and stopping it running too fast.

Steam-engines were expensive to buy and to operate and only the larger and more profitable mines and factories could afford them. Purchasers of the pumping engine paid for it on the basis of the coal saved in comparison with an atmospheric engine: generally the Boulton and Watt engines used a third less coal. The customer erected the engine himself under the guidance of drawings and an engineer from the Soho works. At first they were bought mainly for the Cornish tin and copper mines and the iron mines in Shropshire and Staffordshire, but eventually some were installed in coal mines too.

From the 1780s 60 per cent of the Boulton and Watt Co.'s output consisted of rotary engines, which were supplied to the purchaser and usually transported by canal. In 1795 they opened the Soho Foundry, equipped solely for building these engines. The first rotary engines were used mainly to drive bellows, rollers and hammers in iron works and cotton-spinning machines in mills in Lancashire, Derbyshire and Nottinghamshire. (The first steam-powered mill was set up at Papplewick, near Nottingham in 1785). In 1800 when Boulton and Watt's Patent expired they handed over their business to their sons and retired to live in comfort. By then there were approximately 1,000 steam-engines all over Britain, of which Boulton and Watt had built about half.

Later Developments

During the early nineteenth century steam-engines were used in an increasing range of industries, including flour-milling, brewing, distilling, sugar-refining, paper-making, printing and coin-minting, and in transport too, after Richard Trevithick and others had developed high pressure steam. However, it is easy to exaggerate the rate at which industry adopted steam-engines. By 1830 there were tens of thousands in use, mostly in cotton, but many cotton and most woollen mills still used water power. Until the 1830s steam-engines were individually made without standardized parts so that when they broke down, as often happened, an engineer from the original makers had to repair them. Mass produced steam-engines began to be made in the 1830s and they were widely adopted in woollen mills and most other manufacturing industries during the second half of the nineteenth century.

Steam power enabled industry to grow rapidly and to move away from rivers into towns near the coalfields. It led to iron being made in huge quantities and coal being mined from deep seams, to the growth of engineering and of the machine tool industry and to the development of railways and steamships.

Textiles to 1830s

Domestic System

Woollen cloth-making was the most important British industry in the mid-eighteenth century and only agriculture employed more people. Raw wool from the sheep's backs was transformed into finished cloth by nearly thirty different processes. The two most important ones were spinning and weaving which were normally carried out by women and men respectively in their homes. Other processes like fulling, dressing and dyeing required bigger equipment and were usually done in small workshops. This domestic system was often organized by a middleman or clothier who bought the wool from the farmers and then passed it on at each stage to the different workers before he finally sold the finished cloth. Some wool was produced in all counties, but three regions specialized in making the finer cloths: East Anglia, the West Country and the West Riding of Yorkshire.

Silk

The other main textiles, cotton, linen and silk, were all far less important. The first successful factory had been built in 1717–21 near Derby on the river Derwent, by the brothers John and Thomas Lombe, to make silk with a water-driven machine copied from the Italians. It was 150 metres long, and five storeys high, employed several hundred people and soon made a fortune. Several factories were erected in Stockport, Congleton and Macclesfield, but silk never became a major industry because the cost of its raw material was so high.

Cotton

Cotton and linen making were established in south Lancashire and the lowlands of Scotland. Since it was illegal to make pure cotton goods until the 1770s, cotton and linen were woven together to form a coarse cloth called fustian. Their manufacture was organized in a way similar to wool with some of the finishing processes being done in London. Better quality cotton cloth was imported from India.

Cotton was an attractive material with a wide variety of uses. It washed more easily than wool and was more pleasant to wear next to the skin. As the demand for it increased, several enterprising men were stimulated to devise new ways of producing larger quantities more cheaply.

About 1760 weavers began to take up generally an invention of 1733 which enabled them to weave much wider cloth at nearly four times their normal speed. This was, *John Kay's 'Flying Shuttle'* which was struck from one side of the old-style weaving loom to the other by wooden hammers operated by the weaver. Kay (1704–64), who had been born near Bury in Lancashire, had originally met such opposition from the weavers who feared that unemployment would follow that he left the country and died in France in poverty. The flying shuttle's widespread use in the 1760s led to an increased demand for spun thread which spinners with spinning-wheels were unable to satisfy.

James Hargreaves (1720–78), a Blackburn weaver, devised the first successful spinning machine about 1765. His *'Spinning Jenny'* (patented in 1770) was still operated by hand like a spinning-wheel, but at first it spun eight threads at once and with later improvements eighty or more. Like Kay, Hargreaves faced bitter opposition from spinners fearing unemployment, so he fled to Nottingham. By 1788, 20,000 jennies were being used, mostly in people's homes, but though they spun fine thread it was only strong enough for the weft and not the warp.

.*Richard Arkwright* (1732–92) was a barber and wig-maker who had moved from Preston to Bolton where he soon realized that a fortune could be made from improving the spinning process. In 1769 he patented the *'water-frame'* which used rollers to stretch and spin a fine, strong yarn. This machine which was based on earlier inventions and may well have been pirated, needed power to drive it and had to be installed in a factory. He immediately set up a horse-powered spinning mill in Nottingham and then in 1771 moved to Cromford, where the Derwent flowed swiftly through a narrow gorge near the Lombe's silk mill. Here Arkwright built a similar water-powered factory which was soon turning out large quantities of thread suitable for the warp so that fine cotton cloth could be woven. Arkwright had started to make a huge fortune. He expanded his business by opening new mills in partnership with other wealthy men at Belper, Chorley, Manchester and New Lanark in Scotland. Soon other industrialists followed his example in areas which had fast flowing streams. The factory system had arrived. Arkwright also produced in 1775 a rotary carding machine which prepared the cotton for spinning much more rapidly.

In 1779 **Samuel Crompton** (1753–1827), the son of a small landowner near Bolton, devised a machine which married the strengths of the jenny and water-frame to produce both fine and strong thread and which he called the *'mule'*. But because he could not patent it and because he was no businessman Crompton made very little money from his invention, which enabled British manufacturers to make cotton goods as fine in quality as those from the East. Other inventors improved it so that by the 1790s it was harnessed to water-power and capable of spinning 300 threads or more. (And in 1825 Richard Roberts of Manchester finally produced a very efficient self-acting mule). By the 1830s the price of cotton yarn had fallen by over 90 per cent since the 1780s (from 38 shillings per lb to 3 shillings.)

The speed of **weaving** was now the bottle-neck to further progress in the cotton industry. The loom was such a complex machine that many manufacturers maintained that it was impossible to adapt it to water-power. **The Reverend Edmund Cartwright** (1743–1823) a former tutor at Magdalen College, Oxford, who had never seen a weaver at work, set out to prove them wrong. In 1785 he patented a power loom of sorts but his own attempts to go into business in Doncaster failed, partly because his loom was still too clumsy even after some improvements. He also aroused the anger of the hand-loom weavers who burned down a mill in Manchester that was using his power looms. With so much machine-spun yarn available, the hand-loom weavers were enjoying very high wages which they did not want to see reduced. However, Cartwright had shown that powered looms could be driven by water or steam and their use spread gradually as they were improved. In 1803 John Horrocks of Stockport produced a power loom made of metal and soon more and more plain cloth was being woven in factories.

These developments stimulated technical changes which speeded up the **finishing processes**. In 1784 Thomas Bell patented a machine which used copper rollers to print coloured patterns on lengths of cotton cloth (or calico). Bleaching was a very slow process, using sour milk and sunlight. In 1785 James Watt introduced to England the French discovery of the use of chlorine as a bleaching agent and from 1799 Charles Tennant produced chloride of lime (which was a dry, easily transportable powder) in increasing quantities near Glasgow.

Yet the spread of factories was still a gradual process which had only just begun by 1815. The hand-loom weavers fought in vain against falling prices and by the

1830s cotton production was finally concentrated into mills. Since the machinery was increasingly driven by steam power these mills were no longer built by swift streams but in the towns of South Lancashire, around Manchester, and of Clydeside, near Glasgow, which were close to coal mines. By 1835 90 per cent of the cotton manufacture was produced in Lancashire and its adjacent counties.

The Woollen Industry

This adopted new machinery much more slowly. It was older and more scattered than cotton and its clothiers were less inclined to accept change. Wool was also a softer fibre and tended to break more easily on the early machines. Yorkshire took the lead in using the new machines because it was close to Lancashire and could see their value more clearly. Flying shuttles and spinning-jennies were widely used in Yorkshire by 1790, but still in people's homes. Factories developed first for spinning worsted. The earliest worsted mill was established in 1787 at Addingham near Skipton and from the 1790s Crompton's mule was introduced to mills in Bradford and Leeds. Power looms were not used widely in the weaving of worsted until the 1830s. They were not adopted for the manufacture of other softer woollens until the 1850s, when a successful combing machine was at last devised. Like Lancashire, Yorkshire had many rivers flowing off the Pennines for water power, and rich coalfields for steam power. The traditional woollen centres, such as Norwich, Colchester and Tiverton, declined and were replaced by the Yorkshire towns of Leeds, Bradford, Halifax and Huddersfield.

During the early nineteenth century cotton replaced wool as the country's major textile industry and throughout the century both continued to grow. Many reasons account for the rapid expansion of cotton. They included the natural resources and climate of South Lancashire, the excellence of Liverpool's facilities as a port for imports and exports and of Manchester as a commercial and financial centre, which supported and encouraged those industrialists who were prepared to take risks to meet the rapidly growing world-wide demand for cheap fabrics. And not until the American Civil War (1861–5) was the expansion of the cotton industry held back by a shortage of raw cotton supplies. Until then the invention, in 1793, of Eli Whitney's cotton gin which speeded up the extraction of seeds from raw cotton, had enabled the American grower to meet the British manufacturer's increasing demand for raw cotton at a steadily declining price.

By the 1830s cotton goods manufactured in Britain were cheaper and better than those from elsewhere in the world. Yet the revolution in cotton had been concentrated in Lancashire and Clydeside and it did not have such immediate far-reaching economic effects in Britain as the railways. Nevertheless, it did set a pattern of industrial transformation that was soon to be followed in other industries.

Statistics

Value of textile products (in £ million)		
	1770s	*1830s*
Cotton	1	22
Wool	8	17
Linen	2	5
Silk	1	6
	12	50

Raw cotton consumption (in million lbs)	
1780	8
1830	250
1870	1,100
1910	2,000

Raw wool consumption (in million lbs)	
1800	100
1850	200
1905	700

Numbers employed in cotton (UK) (in thousands)		
	Factory	Hand-loom weavers
1815	115	220
1835	220	190
1855	370	25

Cotton mills 1835			
	Number of mills	Steam horse-power	Water horse-power
Lancashire and adjacent counties	935	26,500	6,100
Scotland	125	3,200	2,500
Midlands	55	450	1,200
	1,115	30,150	9,800

Factories to 1850s

The factory method of production created an entirely new world for those who worked in them. Apart from the golden age of hand-loom weaving, people working under the domestic system had usually been paid so little that everyone, including quite young children, had had to keep working for long hours. They also suffered from bouts of unemployment as well as from having their home full of their instruments of work. And yet they had worked in a familiar environment with people whom they knew, and the family had had some freedom in deciding when they would start and stop work. The factory system profoundly changed their working conditions.

During the later eighteenth century factories caught on comparatively slowly. The use of water power meant that these early factories were often built in remote areas, like Cromford, where the rivers flowed best. From the start, some of these spinning mills were very large. Within four years Arkwright employed 300 people at Cromford and by 1816 his son had nearly 2,000. At the same time some 1,600 were employed by J. Strutt at Belper and the same number by Robert Owen at New Lanark in Scotland. But a survey of 1833 showed that such huge mills were quite exceptional. Out of well over a thousand cotton mills, only seven employed more than 1,000 people and sixty between 250 and 1,000. The steam-driven factories in the towns tended to be much smaller. Altogether nearly a quarter of a million workers were employed in cotton factories by the mid-1830s of whom one in eight were aged under 13, and three in ten aged between 13 and 18.

Factory owners in isolated rural areas were forced to build a whole community with houses, schools and other amenities in addition to their mills. Many of these cotton masters had difficulty in attracting enough workers and so, since much of the work could be done by children, the Poor Law authorities sometimes helped by sending them cartloads of pauper and orphan children. In the towns fewer factory owners accepted responsibility for housing their workers or even looking after them when the work fell off. Outside working hours most 'hands' were left to fend for themselves. During working hours they were at the mercy of the master and his managers.

Factory owners who had invested a lot of money in buildings and machinery were naturally determined to extract the largest possible profit from them. They welcomed the opportunity to be able to supervise their employees at work and kept them working for as long as possible, especially in periods of boom. In winter, gaslight made work possible from long before dawn until well after dark. Except when trade was bad, the hands at first often worked twelve or more hours a day, six days a week, with few breaks. Since no one took naturally to this pattern of work, their employers enforced very strict discipline. Adults who arrived late or neglected their work were often fined, and children were punished physically. Sometimes doors were locked during working hours. To prevent the cotton thread from breaking, windows were kept closed and in hot weather temperatures rose to 30°C or more. The smaller factories were usually the gloomiest and most crowded. Many families also suffered because the children no longer worked with their parents. Even though the early factories normally paid higher and more regular wages, few worked in them willingly. For the masters, one of the main attractions of employing women and children was that they were normally more docile than men.

There were a few enlightened employers who adopted a different attitude to their workers, notably **Robert Owen** (1771–1858) a Welshman who became managing partner of the New Lanark mills on the Clyde in 1800. There he reduced working hours to ten-and-a-half per day, raised wages, which were still paid during sickness or temporary unemployment, stopped children under the age of ten from working and sent them to school instead, built houses with good sanitation, opened shops selling essential goods at cost price: and still made good profits. Many people admired him, but relatively few factory owners imitated him voluntarily even though the development of faster and more powerful machinery from the 1830s made it easier for them to do so. Working conditions were normally worst in the smaller mills where profit margins were smallest.

Factory Acts
The earliest attempts to improve conditions in the cotton factories through Acts passed by Parliament were inspired by some of the best employers and were confined to some of the most vulnerable workers.

The first Sir Robert Peel's **Health and Morals of Apprentices Act, of 1802**, tried to limit the hours of the pauper children to a maximum of twelve a day and to prevent them from working at night, but it was completely ineffective because its enforcement was left to the local magistrates (JPs) who ignored it. This so annoyed Robert Owen that he eventually persuaded the second Sir Robert Peel to set up a committee to inquire into child labour in the cotton factories, but Parliament would not accept any proposals for adequate inspection, so that the **Act of 1819** ineffectively prohibited the employment of children under nine and limited the hours of all under sixteen to twelve a day (and not ten-and-a-half as Owen had wanted).

Abuses of child labour increased with the expansion of factories, until agitation against them was renewed in 1830. The movement for factory reform was sparked off by a letter on 'Yorkshire Slavery', written to the *Leeds Mercury* by Richard Oastler, in which he contrasted William Wilberforce's enthusiasm for the abolition of slavery with his indifference towards the conditions of children working in factories in his constituency. Michael Sadler, who represented the movement in Parliament, introduced a Bill in 1831 to limit the hours of women and children to ten, but it was rejected. Sadler then lost his seat so that Lord Ashley (1801–85), who became Earl of Shaftesbury in 1851, became spokesman for the factory reform movement in Parliament. Outside, it was supported by a few wealthy factory owners, like John Fielden.

Eventually Parliament was shamed into passing the first effective **Factory Act** in **1833**. This established four inspectors to see that its terms were carried out, and their number was later increased. Children aged under nine were prevented from working in all textile mills except silk, and the working day of those between 9 and 13 was reduced to nine hours and of those between 13 and 18 to twelve hours. Also there was to be no night working for those under 18, who were also to have regular breaks for meals. One of the main loopholes of this Act was the difficulty of establishing a child's true age. This was tackled by an Act of **1836** for the **compulsory registration of births**.

The annual reports of the inspectors gave greater publicity to the working conditions in textile factories, which worsened in the slump of the 1840s. Eventually another **Factory Act** was passed in **1844** which reduced the working day of women in textiles to twelve hours and of boys under 13 to six-and-a-half hours so that they might also have half a day's schooling. In addition, dangerous machinery was to be fenced in and machines were not to be cleaned while still in motion. Some employers managed to evade this Act by adopting a shift system so that the factory reform movement continued to press for a ten-hours limit.

In 1847 an Act limited the working day of women and boys and girls under 18 to ten hours, with a maximum working week of fifty-eight hours. In 1850 and 1853 this Act was strengthened by further legislation which restricted the working day for women and under 18s to ten-and-a-half hours, with one-and-a-half hours for meals, but because it set 6.00 a.m. and 6.00 p.m. as the limits it prevented men from working more than twelve hours in textile factories, without actually mentioning them.

Similar provisions were subsequently applied to other industries like bleaching, dyeing, lace-making, pottery and match-making where the working conditions were often even worse than in the textile factories.

Governments were most reluctant to take this action and to accept any responsibility for making sure that people worked in tolerable conditions. These Acts therefore represent an important step in the move away from *'laissez-faire'* towards making those who ran the country accept a wider sense of social responsibility.

Iron to 1840s

Iron-making was Britain's most important metal industry in the mid-eighteenth century, yet the iron-masters could not meet the growing demand for it. Iron was so scarce that people regularly returned nails to their blacksmiths to have them repaired. And so, even though some utensils were made of copper and brass, many things that we would expect to find made of metal were wood.

Because large quantities of charcoal were needed to heat the iron at most stages, the main centres of iron-making had been near wooded areas including the Forest of Dean, South Wales, the Weald of Sussex, Staffordshire, Shropshire and South Yorkshire. All the processes required considerable heat. After the iron ore was smelted in a blast furnace, the molten metal was run off into moulds called 'pigs'. Because this pig-iron still contained many impurities it was brittle though hard. It was either reheated and poured into sand moulds to make objects of cast iron or refined further by repeated reheating and hammering into bars. This purer bar or wrought iron was tough and supple and was used to make nails, guns, chains, locks and many tools: often in forges and workshops near Birmingham. Because there was an increasing shortage of wood, charcoal was scarce and expensive and the country was forced to import more and more bar iron from Sweden.

In less than a hundred years the iron industry was transformed completely. By the early nineteenth century it was playing a vital part in the expansion of the economy, stimulating or making possible the growth of many other industries.

Darbys of Coalbrookdale

There had been various attempts before the eighteenth century to use coal rather than charcoal for making iron, but they had always failed because its sulphorous fumes added impurities to the iron. By 1709 a secretive Quaker iron-founder, Abraham Darby I (1677–1717) of Coalbrookdale in Shropshire, had begun to make cast iron with coal. He used coke made from Shropshire 'clod' coal, which had a small sulphur content, in a larger furnace and with stronger bellows than previously so that the iron was heated at a higher temperature. The hotter pig-iron was also more fluid so that more delicate articles like buttons and cooking utensils which formerly had been made from wrought iron or other metals could be cast in iron. For forty years the process had been confined to Shropshire and not until the 1740s did other iron-masters begin to copy it and make pig-iron more cheaply.

Then in 1749, Abraham Darby II (1711–63) improved upon his father's work by smelting with coke pig-iron suitable for making bar iron of good quality. But charcoal was still needed to reheat the pig-iron for working into bar iron which remained scarce and expensive. In 1766 wrought iron was made at Coalbrookdale in a reverberatory furnace but it was very expensive and later abandoned. But under Abraham Darby III (1750–91) advances continued to be made at Coalbrookdale. Cast-iron rails were made and cast-iron parts for steam-engines and then in 1779 the world's first iron bridge. This was built in collaboration with John Wilkinson near Coalbrookdale across the Severn and led to a small town called Ironbridge growing up beside it.

John Wilkinson (1728–1808), who expanded a small iron foundry founded by his father, married a wealthy wife and soon had numerous iron works, notably round Broseley in Shropshire. There he invented a new lathe for boring cannon more accurately than ever before which also made close fitting pistons and cylinders for Watt's engines. Wilkinson was also the first iron-master to use the steam-engine to blow the blast of his furnaces and to drive the hammers at the forge. He was totally committed to promoting the use of iron, making cast-iron barges, iron pipes to help supply Paris with water and finally a cast-iron coffin for his own burial!

Henry Cort (1740–1800)

In 1783–4, he patented two processes which finally led to the major breakthrough for which the iron industry had been waiting. Together they produced large quantities of cheap wrought iron. Cort, who was born in Lancaster, became an agent for the navy, supplying it with iron for anchors, guns, nails, etc. But because he found it so difficult to get enough bar iron, he decided to try producing it himself. He set up a forge and slitting mills at Fontley, near Fareham, close to Portsmouth, where he united the processes of **puddling and rolling** that had previously been used separately by other iron-masters. The pig-iron was heated in a reverberatory furnace, where the coke was kept separate from the iron and the heat from the fuel was reflected onto the metal from the roof. The molten iron was stirred, or puddled, with long rods which helped burn off the impurities as it cooled. It was then taken in a semi-molten state to be hammered and passed through different grooved rollers which removed the remaining impurities and turned it into bars or plates of wrought iron. Using the puddling and rolling processes good quality wrought iron could now be made fifteen times more quickly without using charcoal, and much more cheaply. Cort made little profit from his work because his partner had obtained money dishonestly and the navy terminated his patents, but the country benefited enormously.

Rails, pipes, ships, machines and a great variety of other objects were soon made of iron and the iron industry became concentrated near coalfields including South Wales, Shropshire, South Yorkshire and central Scotland. The number of blast furnaces in action rose from 30 in 1780 to 300 in 1830 and steam-engines were used increasingly by the iron-works for tasks like driving the bellows in blast furnaces.

Further Developments

The continued expansion of iron production in the first half of the nineteenth century was helped by two further developments. In 1828, **James Neilson** the manager of the Glasgow Gas Works, took out a patent for a **hot blast furnace**. He realized that using a cold air blast reduced the heat in a furnace. By passing the blast pipe through an oven he made the air hot and reduced the fuel consumption substantially, especially when a few years later he used raw coal instead of coke. Then less than one third of the fuel was needed.

In 1839 a Scottish engineer who had settled in Manchester **James Nasmyth** invented the **steam hammer**, which he patented in 1842. This made it possible to forge very large plates and long bars of iron for the first time. His hammer was simply an inverted steam-engine cylinder, fixed on top of a massive iron frame, with a heavy iron head fitted on the end of the piston-rod. Not only could this hammer deliver blows with tremendous force, but the forgeman's control was such that it could be brought down so gently as to rest on the shell of an egg without cracking it. The steam hammer produced huge quantities of iron for the railways almost immediately. It was another development of major importance in Britain's industrial expansion.

Pig-iron output	
(in thousand tons)	
1720	25
1788	69
1806	244
1830	677
1854	3,070

Steel to 1914

Steel is a superior variety of iron. It is an alloy of pure iron and a small amount of other metals and of carbon (less than 2 per cent) that is as hard as cast iron, as pliable as wrought iron and stronger than both. But because it could not be mass-produced until the mid-nineteenth century, it was more expensive than either. As wrought iron became less capable of withstanding the growing stresses of fast-moving machinery and high-pressure steam, the incentives increased to discover a method of mass-producing steel. At first large quantities of inferior steel were made in Germany from the 1840s by stopping the puddling of wrought iron before it was finished. Then steel production was revolutionized in Britain by three inventions between 1856 and 1879 which led to a new phase of industrial development and a massive increase in the output of steel.

Steel output in Britain	
(in thousand tons)	
1850	60
1870	300
1890	3,600
1910	6,400

Long before these developments in mass-produced steel making, **Benjamin Huntsman** (1704–76), a clockmaker from Doncaster, had devised a method of making better steel in the early 1740s. First he had heated bar iron and bits of charcoal together in a furnace to make the traditional blister steel which was then broken up into small pieces. These were placed with scraps of shear steel and a special flux, mostly of charcoal, in closed fire-clay crucibles, about 25 cm high. Then they were melted by intense heat in coke-fired furnaces to produce cast steel of a very high and even quality. This was used for making mainly clock and watch springs, sharp knives and razors. Huntsman then moved to Sheffield where his method of steel making was soon used by other firms.

Sir Henry Bessemer (1813–98)
Over a hundred years later this professional inventor, who was trying to make improved cannons during the Crimean war, patented in 1856 his **converter** for mass producing cheaper steel. After pouring several tons of molten pig-iron into an egg-shaped furnace or converter, he burned off the impurities by blasting heated air through it from the bottom for about twenty minutes. He then added the appropriate quantities of manganese, containing carbon, to make mild steel. While still

molten it was tipped into a huge ladle and poured into ingots. At first Bessemer's method often failed. Later he realized that it did not work when the iron ore contained substantial quantities of phosphorus. Nevertheless the output of steel from more expensive non-phosphoric ores increased, its price fell and Bessemer soon made a huge fortune. Bessemer's invention was as revolutionary for steel-making as Cort's processes had been for making wrought iron.

William Siemens (1823–83)

The second major invention to transform steel-making did not solve the problem of phosphoric ores but it did make better steel more cheaply. During the 1860s, William Siemens, a German engineer who had settled in England, developed the *Open Hearth* process, which he patented in 1866. By this method the hot blast of air and gaseous fuel was heated by waste gases from the furnace before it passed over a shallow bath of pig-iron where it burned out the impurities. But it was not used for successful steel making until a Frenchman, Pierre Martin, discovered that different quantities of scrap iron had to be placed in the bath with the pig-iron according to the qualities of the ore. Because it was easier to control the open hearth than the Bessemer process it could be used to make the better quality steel needed for shipbuilding and so the open hearth process caught on faster in Britain than in other industrial countries.

Sidney Gilchrist Thomas (1850–85)

The problem of phosphoric ores was finally solved by the *basic process*, invented in 1878–9 by Sidney Gilchrist Thomas, a London policecourt's clerk who had studied metallurgy at evening classes, and his cousin Percy Gilchrist who was a chemist at a Welsh ironworks. Together they devised a method which put basic limestone in the molten iron and lined the furnace with basic matter to absorb and draw off the phosphorus. This comparatively simple development which could be applied to both converters and open hearths made them instantly world famous, because, like Britain's, most of the world's iron ore contained phosphorus. It further reduced the cost of steel which from the 1880s finally began to replace wrought iron in most structural uses for railways, bridges, ships, boilers, guns, and all kinds of machines. The combined use of steel and concrete—reinforced concrete—also led to important changes in building construction.

Changes in steel-making came very rapidly during the second half of the nineteenth century. The Bessemer and Siemens-Martin processes led to steel works developing near the ports in South Wales, Middlesborough and the Clyde valley because huge quantities of phosphorus free iron ore had to be imported. Britain's only non-phosphoric ironfield was also developed in Cumberland. And because British steel makers were slower to adopt the Gilchrist Thomas process than many of their German and American rivals, by the beginning of the twentieth century Britain no longer led the world in steel production. In addition, almost all developments in the production of high quality steel alloys took place abroad. A new era had begun in which Britain's economic supremacy would be challenged successfully.

Guide to Questions

The types of questions set on this section will vary a great deal, but you are certain to have at least one of them in your examination, and possibly more than one. Most questions are descriptive, although some do involve explanations as well. Steam power questions usually go up to about 1830, and fall into three categories: 1) asking for an explanation of the uses of steam power; 2) how important steam was to the development of industry; and 3) the significance of Boulton and Watt. Some questions ask for knowledge of the steam-engines themselves, e.g. *Describe the various improvements to steam-engines that were made during the eighteenth century. In what ways did these improved engines prove useful?* (London, 1980). Beware of the temptation to turn your account into a technical exercise.

The textile questions are mostly between 1760 and 1820 and deal either with changes in the methods of production and the impact on the lives of those concerned, or with an explanation of why cotton overtook wool, e.g. *Outline the main changes which occurred in the production of cotton in the eighteenth century* (London, 1979), and *Why did the cotton industry grow more rapidly than the woollen industry in the late eighteenth and early nineteenth centuries?* (Southern, 1976). Sometimes, 'short notes' questions are asked, involving the main eighteenth-century inventions (and occasionally the inventors too), but the essay questions are either 'describe' or 'explain'.

The factory questions deal with nineteenth-century working conditions in textile mills, and you are expected to know about conditions before 1850, and their reform, e.g. *Imagine you were one of the early factory inspectors. Describe factory conditions as you found them in 1834 and how they had been improved by 1850* (Oxford, 1979). Candidates often assume that factory owners were deliberately cruel, except for Robert Owen, so sometimes questions are set comparing the domestic system with work in the mills. Questions show that you are expected to know the main facts about the most important Factory Acts, Robert Owen, and Lord Shaftesbury.

Questions on iron normally cover the period up to about 1830, and mostly expect a description of the changes in methods of production, sometimes with an explanation, e.g. *Account for and describe the development and expansion of the iron industry between 1760 and 1830* (Oxford, 1976). There are 'short notes' questions here, too, including biographies of Cort, Wilkinson, and Neilson. Occasionally, steel is also included but you only need something on Huntsman and a comment on the expense of steel before the 1850s. The nineteenth century steel questions are mainly 'describe and explain' and generally cover 1850–1914. They usually expect a knowledge of how steel production increased and the effect this had upon the economy. Sometimes this involves a biography-style question, sometimes a collection of statistics.

The five question plans provide a cross-section of those you could face: one 'describe'; one 'explain'; one biography; one 'imagine'; and one 'describe and explain'.

Specimen Question 1
In which industries was the steam-engine used in the period from 1750 to about 1830? What difficulties had to be overcome by builders and users of steam-engines in this period? (Southern, 1979)

It makes sense to deal with the difficulties first, since the steam-engine could not be widely used until they had been solved. After the 1780s, steam was used more widely, and the plan refers to three major industries to show this. Each of them should be dealt with in a separate paragraph, which also needs an explanation of the difficulties in using steam power in that industry. Do not give the impression that steam-engines were used at every mill, furnace, etc., by 1830.

Suggested essay plan *Introduction* Alternative sources of power unsatisfactory by 1750. Atmospheric engine had already been developed by Newcomen.

1 Difficulties Costly, inefficient, only reciprocal. Watt's separate condenser and other improvements of the 1780s did much to resolve this.

2 Industries Steam power used increasingly during period of question, but especially so in three industries:

a) *Mining* Principal use: pumping water from coal mines. Only profitable mines could afford them: running costs and maintenance.

b) *Iron* Used after 1775 i) to provide blast in furnace ii) to operate hammers at forge iii) to operate rollers (after 1784). Demand for steam-engines helped iron industry to grow. Until 1780s difficult to control speed: largest firms only: expense.

c) *Cotton* After Papplewick, 1785, growth of spinning mills, then weaving mills too. By 1830 most produced by mills and wool starting to mechanize. Larger firms only: smaller ones still used water-wheels.

Conclusion Most important source of power for the 'Industrial Revolution' 1780–1830. But 'Age of Steam' not until after 1850.

Specimen Question 2

Why did the cotton industry grow more rapidly than the woollen industry in the late eighteenth and early nineteenth centuries? (Southern, 1976)

An 'explain' question which is not easy to plan, since the temptation is to devote most of the essay to a description of the machinery used in the period. There are five main machines, but do not describe them in detail, since the question does not require it; do try to explain the effect they had. The dates of the question are roughly 1770–1820, and you need to beware of suggesting that the introduction of the factory system in cotton explains this change. Factories were not widespread until after the 1820s.

Suggested essay plan *Introduction* Before 1770s wool most prosperous textile. By early nineteenth century surpassed by cotton: 'the wonder of the age'.

1 Cotton advantages a) Attractive material, easy to wear and wash. b) Previous restrictions on cotton removed by 1770s. c) Increased demand from growing population: declining price.

2 Availability Especially after Whitney's cotton gin. Imported via Liverpool; production concentrated in South Lancashire. Increased demand and availability of raw material meant a readiness to adopt improved techniques. (NB wool traditional and conservative.) Cotton thread coped better with machinery than wool.

3 Spinning Hargreaves and Crompton for domestic use. Arkwright: beginning of cotton mills: not widespread until 1820s.

4 Weaving Cartwright and Horrocks. Not widely used until the 1820s.

Conclusion Variety of reasons; cotton more enterprising than wool and more adaptable.

Specimen Question 3

Describe the career of Anthony Ashley Cooper, 7th Earl of Shaftesbury (1801–85) and assess his importance as a social reformer. (Oxford, 1973)

Occasionally, you will come across questions which deal just with the life of one person, like Edwin Chadwick or George Stephenson. Most biographical questions are of the 'short notes' type, but this question on Shaftesbury is a 'describe and explain' essay.

It is often a temptation to write a biography chronologically, but there are other ways of doing it. Here, his career has been broken down into three main sections. Shaftesbury is mentioned in the text, but not in detail, so extra information about him is included in this essay plan.

Suggested essay plan *Introduction* Connected with wide variety of social reforms from 1820s. Came from a respected and influential family.

1 Background Strong moral views; very religious: Evangelical. Became MP in 1826. Appointed to Select Committee on Pauper Lunatics: turning point in his life. Retained concern for the mentally handicapped for the rest of his life.

2 Factory reform a) 1833: Sadler had lost seat: Ashley last resort: took up cause with great enthusiasm. Campaigned for 1833, 1844 and 1850 Acts: out of Parliament when 1847 Act passed. b) Helped to publicize conditions in factories, especially for women and children; contacts with government circles aided movement for reform.

3 Children a) Shocked by 1842 Royal Commission: supported Mines Act. Ragged Schools Union, 1844; Climbing Boys Society; Shoeblacks; Factories also. b) Promoted awareness of abuses of child labour through his speeches inside and outside Parliament. His public standing meant that these abuses received even more attention.

4 Public health a) Was Commissioner at Board of Health 1848–54; closely associated with Chadwick: graveyards, water supply, slum clearance, working class housing. Tried to smoothe differences between Chadwick and his colleagues. b) Again, played an important part in popularizing these conditions.

Conclusion Gave great publicity to the causes he supported. Very energetic, sincere, and with important family links.

Specimen Question 4

Assume it is 1780 in Coalbrookdale, Shropshire. A visitor has arrived from London to see the new iron bridge. You are an old man of eighty who has lived in the area all his life and who worked for many years for the Darby family. Write a conversation between yourself and the visitor in which you describe the changes you have seen while working for the Darbys. (AEB, 1977)

There are enough clues in the wording of the question for you to be able to plan your answer. The time span is from about 1710 to 1780, and the question is obviously an 'imagine' style one, so avoid the temptation to write a descriptive answer about the iron industry. The essay plan outlines one way of presenting this conversation: in terms of the problems the old man remembers and how they were eventually solved; and then the iron bridge was built, a symbol of the new age of iron. More than in most other questions, you have to consider carefully how you would write this type of answer: you could easily come across such a question in other parts of the course.

Suggested essay plan *Introduction* Meeting with the London visitor. Ironbridge already tourist centre by 1780. Visitor interested in growth of iron industry in area.

1 Problem of fuel   Shortcomings of charcoal: discoveries of Abraham Darby I and II, using local 'clod' coal. Locals become used to the sight of coke pits. Growth of Darby firm; products made.

2 Problem of power   For blast and hammers. Steam used after 1775; pistons and cylinders made at Coalbrookdale. The size and the smell of the larger furnaces.

3 Problem of transport   Increase in amount of traffic using the River Severn in his lifetime; raw materials and finished products: trade carried on far and wide.

4 Ironbridge   Typifies new age: Abraham Darby III and Wilkinson. What is the world coming to? Darby family and their Company world famous: who would have thought it?

Conclusion   Vast changes during lifetime. Rise of the Coalbrookdale Iron Company as one of the greatest in the country.

Specimen Question 5

Describe the changes in the methods of the production of steel between 1850 and 1900. What effects did these changes have on the British economy? (Southern, 1978)

A two-part question in the 'describe and explain' category. Your answer should make two things clear: 1) The methods of production: the processes of 1856, 1866–7 and 1879. The plan divides them into two paragraphs, since the Bessemer and Siemens-Martin processes only worked with non-phosphoric ores. 2) The effects of these changes, based on the uses for steel after the 1870s, together with the rise of foreign competition.

Suggested essay plan   *Introduction*   Before 1850 production small-scale and expensive. Iron widely used.

1 Methods   a) **Bessemer and Siemens-Martin processes.** Include details of both processes. Point out that they could only be used with non-phosphoric ores. b) **Gilchrist Thomas process.** Include details. Solved the problem of the use of all types of ores.

2 Effects   a) Uses of steel by 1880s. b) Foreign competition: Gilchrist Thomas process widely used in Germany and the USA; therefore it proved to be the basis for foreign competition: they had overtaken British steel production by 1914.

Conclusion   Great period of expansion: 'the Age of Steel'. But it led to growth of foreign competition too.

Chapter 4 *Transport 1750–1914*

As trade and industry expanded and agriculture flourished, and the population grew especially in the towns, merchants, manufacturers and farmers needed more and more an efficient transport system. In 1750, the methods of transport available had remained virtually unchanged for centuries, except for minor developments. For people, the fastest means of travelling was on horseback, but few could afford a horse. Most had to walk. Most goods were moved in carts or by packhorses. Where possible, heavy goods were sent by boat down rivers and round the coast. Few journeys covered much more than thirty miles in one day and goods rarely travelled at more than 2 or 3 miles an hour.

Roads to 1850

Most roads were no more than cart tracks, inferior in quality to those made by the Romans. Since 1555 each parish had been responsible for the upkeep of its own roads. It appointed annually a Surveyor of the Highways to superintend the work, but normally he had no special knowledge and most parishioners did little to help on their six statutory days, even when they did appear. Parishes on main roads particularly resented having to provide for non-local traffic and the condition of these roads was often deplorable. Since 1706 Parliament's response to this problem had been to set up **turnpike trusts**.

Turnpike trusts were run by groups of trustees who took over responsibility for a short stretch of main road (perhaps 10–15 miles), which they cordoned off with gates, and charged the user tolls to pay for repairs to the road. Most trustees were local landowners whose interests were served by improved roads. But since no one supervised them some were dishonest, inefficient, and neglected the roads and concentrated on collecting the tolls, which made them very unpopular. However, most contributed to maintaining the roads. Many more improved the worst bits, widening the road where it was too narrow, making more easily graded stretches on steep hills and building bridges across rivers.

Their biggest problem was to keep adequately repaired the busiest roads between the large towns and those which crossed the heavy claylands, e.g. the Weald and the South-east Midlands. Drainage was the main problem and loads of stones or gravel dropped into deep ruts and pot-holes could soon be churned into mud again by heavy wagons. Parliament tried to help by encouraging heavy wagons to have broad nine-inch wheels in 1753, and axles of different length in 1765, but such measures proved quite ineffective. The solution lay in constructing better road surfaces.

John Metcalf (1717–1810)
Metcalf was one of the first engineers to apply scientific principles to road building. Although blind from the age of six, he was a busy carrier based on Knaresborough in Yorkshire, when a trust asked him in 1765 to build three miles of road near Harrogate. This was so successful that until 1792 he was employed to build another

180 miles, mainly across the Pennines in Yorkshire and Lancashire. His method was to lay a firm foundation of big stones and use smaller ones to build up a smooth, convex surface with deep ditches on either side for drainage. On boggy moorland he achieved a firm foundation by first laying bundles of heather.

Thomas Telford (1757–1834)

Telford was a professional civil engineer who built, mainly in Scotland, canals, harbours and bridges as well as roads. From 1786 he was also employed as Surveyor of Roads in Shropshire, but his greatest work as a road builder was on the **London to Holyhead road**, especially in the stretch from Shrewsbury into North Wales, which he began in 1815 and completed fifteen years later. After the Act of Union with Ireland this was politically one of the most important roads linking Dublin with London. Telford's method of construction was not unlike Metcalf's but his foundations were more solid, he had a four centimetre layer of gravel on the top, his camber was less, his drainage system more elaborate and his gradients never more than one in forty. He also spanned the Menai Straits with a magnificent suspension bridge. Altogether, the government spent about £750,000 on improving this road and building Holyhead harbour. Few turnpike trusts could afford to pay for work of such quality.

John Loudon McAdam (1756–1836)

McAdam was another Scotsman who devised a cheaper and easier method of making roads. He concentrated on drainage rather than solid foundations and used the idea of a French engineer to show that if a bed of small stones no more than thirteen centimetres in diameter was laid on dry soil and covered with smaller stones, a waterproof crust would be formed by the moving traffic which kept out both water and frost. In 1816 he became General Surveyor to the Bristol turnpike trust (with 150 miles of road) and by 1823 he had advised thirty-two others and his three sons eighty-five more. His method of construction cost about £88 per mile and under his supervision over 1,000 miles of road was laid down. (NB These surfaces were not covered with tar asphalt—'tar macadam'—before the 1860s.) Because they had grown up haphazardly, McAdam also encouraged the turnpike trusts to merge into larger units.

Wagon Services

In the later eighteenth century, caravans of packhorses and mules died out in all but the hilliest and remotest parts of the country. They were displaced by a rapidly expanding network of wagon services which were run over long and short distances by many carriers. These wagons, which were great lumbering vehicles, were normally pulled by four to eight horses and moved at a slow walking pace. They carried practically anything, including passengers, and charged about one shilling per ton per mile, but it did vary a lot according to the type of goods. They had regular time-tables and by 1835, for instance, a substantial firm like Pickford's ran six wagons daily on the forty-mile route from Manchester to Sheffield. By then over 800 public carriers operated from London and one Directory listed more than 14,000 regular wagon services each week throughout the whole country.

Stage Coaches

Passenger travel increased even more on the roads after they were improved. In the mid-eighteenth century, London had been linked to most major provincial towns by regular coach services, but they did not run very frequently until at least the 1780s. For example, one coach a week ran between London and Birmingham in 1740, and thirty by 1783.

The coaches rarely carried more than four passengers inside and a dozen outside. The routes were divided into stages of between five and fifteen miles. Each stage ended at an inn where the horses were changed and stabled and the passengers could alight. It was illegal for the horses to gallop, but if only one of the four which pulled the coach trotted, the law was not broken.

The appearance of **mail coaches** in the 1780s gave a great boost to coach travel. They were devised by a Bath theatre manager, **John Palmer**, to replace the slower and rather unreliable system of post boys on horseback. With a limited number of passengers inside only and an armed guard outside, they were exempt from tolls and soon ran regularly and safely at an average speed of eight miles an hour. The first service was introduced in 1784 between London and Bristol and was so successful that mail coaches were soon running on all main roads. By the early nineteenth century most towns had a daily delivery of letters and trade and industry greatly benefited.

The other stage coaches were also stimulated to try to rival the mail coaches. It took skill and smooth organization as well as better roads to keep the coaches running at average speeds of 9 to 10 miles an hour; but this was achieved by the early nineteenth century, when the travelling times for most journeys were about a fifth or a quarter of those in the mid-eighteenth century. In 1750, for instance, it took coaches four days in summer to reach York from London, but only twenty hours by 1836.

Travelling by coach was never cheap. By the 1830s fares were approximately 3d per mile outside and nearly double inside and tips and meals added considerably to the cost. Nevertheless, there was a great boom in coach travel in the 1820s and 1830s. By 1829, for example, 34 a day were running between London and Birmingham. During the 1830s a total of 3,000 stage coaches were licensed in the country, employing 150,000 horses and 30,000 men.

Then, in the 1840s, mail and stage coaches were finished as a method of long distance transport. Neither could compete with the railways.

Canals to 1850

Navigable Rivers
Moving heavy, bulky goods on eighteenth-century roads was clumsy, slow and very expensive. Therefore, coal, iron ore and other minerals were rarely sent more than ten to twenty miles overland. The nearest coal mine to the city of York was sixteen miles away, but its coal still came from Newcastle-upon-Tyne over 200 miles away, round the coast and up the Humber estuary and the River Ouse. From Horsehay near Coalbrookdale to Chester is less than sixty miles by road, yet iron was sent there in 1775 down the River Severn to Bristol, and then round all the coast of Wales: a journey of over 400 miles. Londoners got all their coal by sea from Newcastle and much of their grain by barge down the River Thames. Britain was fortunate to be an island with a long coastline that was connected to useful estuaries and many miles of navigable rivers. In England five river systems covered much of

the country: those flowing into the Mersey and Wash as well as the Humber, Severn and Thames. By 1750 they had been made navigable as high up as possible by dredging, cutting out bends and building locks by weirs. Together they formed the chief highway for the movement of heavy goods. And yet, there were many areas which did not have easy access to these rivers or the coast.

Early Canals

The obvious solution to these difficulties was to cut artificial waterways, or canals. These were no new idea, since several had already been constructed in France and elsewhere. In Britain, the chief incentive for the building of the first short canals was the rapidly growing demand in industrial towns for coal. In 1757, the ten-mile Sankey Navigation linked the St. Helens coalfield to the Mersey, and so with Liverpool. Four years later, a more famous ten-mile canal was opened, connecting the Duke of Bridgewater's Worsley mines with Manchester. The idea for the canal came from the Duke's estate manager who realized that it would also draw off flood water from the mine. To reach Manchester, the canal had to cross the River Irwell and two bogs. It took two years to construct, and the Duke took all the financial risks himself.

James Brindley (1716–72)

Brindley was the engineer in charge of the building of the Bridgewater Canal. He was a self-taught millwright from near Buxton in Derbyshire, who had already built a tunnel near Worsley to take water to a water-wheel. To keep the water in the canal, he lined its banks with clay, puddled with water, and he also designed an aqueduct twelve metres high to carry it over the Irwell. The canal was such a success, reducing the price of coal in Manchester by half, that the Duke of Bridgewater immediately planned a twenty-four-mile extension to Runcorn on the Mersey. It was virtually completed by 1767, except for a flight of ten locks to link it to the river. Legal and financial difficulties delayed its opening for nine years, until after Brindley was dead.

By then, he had been involved in planning the building of about 300 miles of important canals in the Midlands, but the demand for his services was so great that he could not give them all his personal attention, and not all were finished by 1772. Indeed, Brindley had talked of a *'Grand Cross'* which would connect the rivers linking Liverpool and London, Hull and Bristol, in the form of a St. Andrew's cross. This was completed in 1790.

The canals with which Brindley was associated were:

1   The Grand Trunk Canal   which joined the rivers Trent and Mersey. It was 93 miles long and was opened in 1777 after taking 11 years to build. As well as carrying coal and iron, it supplied the Potteries with raw materials (china clay and flint stone) and took away their fragile finished goods. Josiah Wedgwood was a principal shareholder. Brindley's major engineering problem was the 1⅔-mile long Hare-castle tunnel.

2   The Staffordshire and Worcestershire (opened in 1772) branched off from the Grand Trunk to the River Severn at Stourport. It linked the ironworks of Shropshire to the Black Country.

3   The Birmingham Canal (completed 1772) connected this thriving iron and brass manufacturing town to the Staffordshire and Worcestershire (and so to Liverpool, Hull and Bristol) and it soon became the centre of the Midland canals.

4 The Oxford Canal (opened in 1790) which linked the Grand Trunk to the Thames (via the Coventry Canal) took such a long time to complete because of financial problems.

The engineering methods which Brindley used on these canals greatly influenced other canal builders. Where possible, he concentrated the locks together and had long, winding routes in between, which followed the contours. He used embankments and cuttings as little as possible. Like nearly all the canals in the Midlands, these were built with narrow 7-feet locks. In the north, south, and South Wales, the locks were usually much wider.

Canal Mania

These canals were so profitable that in the early 1790s there was a rush to make many more. By 1810, over 200 more Canal Acts had been passed, but their value was limited because all did not have the same sized locks. In addition, many were unprofitable because they were built too close to others, or because they went through agricultural regions, like the south of England, where there was insufficient traffic. Telford's first canal, for instance, the Ellesmere in North Wales, opened in 1805, was most impressive technically, with two very fine aqueducts, but it was an economic failure.

At the same time, many important canals were also opened. They included the *Grand Junction* in 1805, which ran directly from Birmingham to London, and the *Kennet and Avon*, which linked the Severn and the Thames, in 1810. In the north of England, it took 46 years to complete the 127-mile long *Leeds and Liverpool Canal* across the Pennines, and it was not opened until 1816. In South Wales, the canals played an essential part in developing the coal and iron fields. Although some of the early canals continued to be shortened, such as the Oxford Canal, the great building was over by 1830. Altogether, the rivers of England and Wales had been supplemented by some 2,600 miles of canals. They supplied water-transport to areas which had previously lacked it, like the Black Country and the Potteries, and linked London to the main industrial areas.

Finance

Even though they were dug by hand and the soil moved in wheelbarrows, canals were expensive to build, costing a total of over £20 million. Money was needed to obtain the Act of Parliament, buy land, survey, pay the engineers and navvies, and buy all the materials. For the early canals, it was supplied mainly by local landowners and businessmen, but later it also came from doctors, parsons, tradesmen, widows and bankers eager for profits.

Uses

Passenger boats were run on a few canals, especially in Scotland, but they were mainly concerned with goods traffic. The average capacity of a narrow boat was 30 tons, but the largest vessels could carry 80–100 tons. From the towpath, a horse could pull about 50 tons, in contrast to 2 tons at most on a road. The canals were run like water roads, with anyone who owned a suitable boat being able to use them, so long as they paid their tolls. Cargoes were charged by the ton per mile, and were generally two-thirds to three-quarters less than road haulage. Coal was by far the most important single commodity carried by the canals. It was essential for feeding steam-engines and blast furnaces, and warming people in towns. They also carried a wide range of other bulky goods, including limestone, iron and other metals, stone for road-making, bricks, timber and slates for building, cotton, wool, salt, corn, flour and beer, as well as a wide range of manufactured goods and their raw materials.

Difficulties and Decline
By the 1830s, the economy had expanded so much that the principal canals were very congested, which often contributed to water shortages, especially in summer. In cold winters, they also iced over. In addition, most boats from the north were too wide to use the narrow canals in the Midlands, nor were they designed to cater for steam-powered boats. Therefore, when the railways appeared, most canal users welcomed their faster and more efficient service. But canals did not decline as rapidly as the stage coaches. As late as the 1880s, they still carried considerable quantities of bulky commodities, but mainly over short distances.

Railways 1825–1914

It is certainly possible to argue that the creation of a railway system was the single most important development in nineteenth-century Britain. By the 1830s, the main roads and canals were barely coping with the demands placed upon them, and over long distances their fastest average speeds were 10 miles an hour by coach and 2 miles an hour by canal. In less than a generation, the railways could move much larger quantities of goods and people much more rapidly to virtually all centres of population in the country. And so the railways contributed to further large-scale economic expansion.

Development of Rails
Wooden railed ways had been used in the seventeenth century, mainly by coal mines near Newcastle-upon-Tyne, so that carts laden with coal could be moved more easily by horses or men to the nearest stretch of navigable water. A rim on the inside of the rails stopped the carts slipping off, and from the later eighteenth century they were made of cast iron. In the early nineteenth century, the rim or flange was placed on the wheels rather than the rails, which were laid on sleepers, usually 4 feet 8½ inches apart. In 1820, **John Birkinshaw** patented stronger wrought iron rails which could carry heavier loads more smoothly; they were known as Bedlington rails after the place in Northumberland where he lived.

Locomotives
Even James Watt refused to believe that moving steam-engines would ever be developed to pull wagons on either roads or rails. Because steam-engines seemed so heavy and cumbersome, he discouraged William Murdock from trying to develop a locomotive. Other engineers experimented with high-pressure steam which made them lighter and more efficient. In 1804, **Richard Trevithick** built a locomotive which pulled ten tons of iron ore for five miles near Merthyr Tydfil in South Wales. Four years later he exhibited another one on a circular track in London, but he soon lost interest, and engineers in the north-east developed the locomotive. In 1813, William Hedley built the *Puffing Billy* and next year George Stephenson the greatly superior *Blucher*.

George Stephenson (1781–1848)

Stephenson was the son of a colliery foreman in Northumberland. As a young man he had a succession of pit jobs and learned a lot about Watt steam-engines. In 1812 he was made engine-wright at Killingworth colliery, and two years later he produced his first locomotive to carry coals to the Tyne six miles away. In 1822, he persuaded the directors of a recently formed company, that was building a 27-mile railed way from the Darlington collieries to the sea at Stockton, to make it suitable for locomotives. Stephenson surveyed the line and supervised the laying of the track which was opened in 1825. Initially, it was run like a turnpiked road with private wagons and coaches being pulled by horses or locomotives.

Liverpool to Manchester   In 1826, Stephenson started to build a double-track railway of 34 miles from Liverpool to Manchester. In the next four years he overcame enormous engineering difficulties, using methods which had been developed by some road and canal builders. He floated the track on rafts of heather and brushwood across Chat Moss, which was up to 9 metres deep in mud; crossed the Sankey Brook with a viaduct 21 metres high; and at the Liverpool end made a very deep cutting through sandstone and a tunnel down to the dock. The question of locomotion was settled by a competition at Rainhill in 1820 which was won by the *Rocket*, with an average speed of 16 miles an hour. Designed by **Robert Stephenson** (1803–59), George's son, it proved to be the ancestor of the modern locomotive, with multiple tubes carrying the hot gases from the furnace through the boiler, and twin pistons coupled directly to the driving wheels. After a ceremonial opening by the Duke of Wellington in September 1830, the Liverpool and Manchester Railway was immediately successful like the Bridgewater Canal. Already by 1831 it was carrying over 1,000 passengers a day and it was making bigger profits from carrying people than goods. Since it was operated exclusively by the company which owned it, the Liverpool and Manchester was effectively the first modern railway.

Early Railways

For a few years, people waited to see if the success of the Liverpool and Manchester would last before they plunged into the costly business of building long main lines and buying off the opposition. George Stephenson did not build another railway, but many listened to his advice, and his son Robert, who had worked closely with his father, proved to be an even better civil engineer. In 1833, Parliament approved the **London and Birmingham** (engineered by Robert Stephenson and opened in 1838) and the **Grand Junction** which would link Birmingham with Liverpool and Manchester. Then, approval for the **London and Southampton** in 1834 and the **Great Western** (London to Bristol) took place in 1835. These were followed by a feverish rush to extend railways in all directions in 1836–7, when Parliament authorized new companies intending to build a total of 1,500 miles of railway. By 1843, over 2,000 miles were operating. Their layout was totally unplanned and they depended entirely on the initiative of a large number of small private companies.

Some towns, such as Derby, suffered from damaging competition between rival companies, while other areas, like most of Wales and Scotland, waited for their first railway, and all the traffic between London and the north had to go through Rugby. Like the canals, these early railways were also built with different widths, with the Great Western using I. K. Brunel's gauge of 7 feet, the Eastern counties 5 feet, and most of the rest Stephenson's 4 feet 8½ inches.

Government intervention The early railways encountered strong opposition from those with financial interests in canals and coaches and from many landowners over whose land they wanted to build. At first, the government took no positive action and intervened only to limit maximum fares and protect the interests of the landowners. Then, in 1844, Parliament rejected Gladstone's attempt to give the government more control over the management of the railways, but it did pass an important Act which compelled the companies to carry third-class passengers at a minimum of 12 miles an hour for no more than a penny a mile on at least one train a day on most lines. A further Act in 1846 prohibited any more broad-gauge lines (but the Great Western did not abandon it finally until 1892).

Railway Mania
Another frenzied burst of activity in 1845–8 led to Parliament passing some 650 Railway Acts, authorizing nearly 9,000 miles of new line. By the early 1850s, therefore, a national network had appeared in England, with London at the centre linked to almost all important towns, and the travelling time between most major cities had been reduced to a few hours. The railways were extended more slowly into Wales and Scotland. Later in the century, many branch lines were built in the country, and some main lines shortened by major engineering feats like the 4¼-mile Severn tunnel. More suburban lines were created in the big towns, especially London, where the underground was started in 1863 but not electrified until the 1890s.

Building railways was a massive undertaking, including the creation of numerous stations, bridges, viaducts, tunnels and embankments. Difficult, dirty and dangerous work, it employed about 50,000 navvies annually from 1830 to 1870, with over a quarter of a million at its peak in 1847.

As the railway network grew, the smaller companies which had originally built the tracks, were merged into bigger units. The first amalgamation was in 1844, when the Midland Railway was formed from the three companies which met at Derby. It was carried out by *George Hudson* (1800–71), a tradesman from York. Knowing nothing about the technology of railways, Hudson used his financial flair to gain control within four years of nearly 1,500 miles of railway by encouraging more amalgamations and investment. But he soon over-reached himself. In 1849, Hudson's dealings were proved to be dishonest and he was forced to resign. However, the policy of amalgamations continued, and by the early twentieth century all the important trunk routes were controlled by fourteen large private companies.

Later Developments
During the later nineteenth century the railways developed in many other ways. From the 1870s, steel rails replaced iron ones. The black signalling system which divided the line into sections and allowed only one train in each at a time, made travelling safer and faster. So did the introduction of vacuum brakes and improvements in the design of locomotives, including the introduction of large bogie wheels. By 1900, some expresses were running at average speeds of 50 miles an hour. Passenger trains became more comfortable, with steam heating, glass in the windows of third-class carriages, better upholstery, lavatories, corridors and restaurant cars. In 1872, the Midland Company put third-class carriages on all its trains, and the other companies soon followed. From the 1860s in London, cheap

early morning and evening trains were run for workmen. Cheap day excursion trains to the seaside became very popular after the introduction of bank holidays from the 1870s.

	Miles of track (Great Britain)	Number of passenger journeys (millions)	Tons of freight carried (millions)
1850	6,000	70	30
1870	13,000	320	150
1890	17,300	800	300
1910	20,000	1,280	500

Effects

Railways affected most aspects of life by the later nineteenth century. Their huge consumption of coal and iron greatly stimulated both industries. They carried raw materials and finished goods for most manufacturing industries. After 1840, they contributed to the setting up of a cheap, fast and efficient postal system from which businessmen greatly benefited. They created employment and encouraged both engineering exports and increased investment in industry.

Railways supported the rapid growth of towns by bringing in food from the countryside as well as people looking for work. From the suburbs they carried commuters. Seaside resorts like Blackpool and Southend grew up and so did special railway towns like Crewe and Swindon.

Guide to Questions

You are very likely to get some kind of transport question in your examination, and most boards ask far more questions on railways than on roads or canals. The railway questions are usually split into two types as far as content is concerned: those dealing with before 1850, and those between 1850 and 1914. Up to 1850, you are usually asked to describe the building of the early railways, the problems faced by the engineers and to explain why these lines were built, e.g. *Describe the development of railways in Britain in the period 1830–50. What difficulties faced the early railway builders?* (Southern, 1978). After 1850, the questions are more general, dealing with the impact of the railways upon the economy and society, e.g. *In what ways had the growth of railways affected a) industry b) agriculture, and c) everyday life by the end of the nineteenth century?* (London, 1979). Most are 'describe and explain', or 'describe' questions, although there are some 'explain' as well. Stimulus and 'imagine' questions are also asked, as are ones including the two Stephensons and Hudson.

Questions on roads are either 'describe' or 'describe and explain', and cover the eighteenth century, and up to about 1830. Some of them are biographical, dealing with the work of the road improvers, especially Telford and McAdam. Others are more general questions on road improvements, e.g. *Describe the main improvements made to the roads of Britain in the period 1750 to 1820. Why was improvement necessary and what effects did it have?* (Southern, 1979). The examiners expect you to know about the engineers and the turnpike trusts.

Questions on canals are mainly 'describe and explain', with a few 'explain', and usually cover the period 1760 to 1830. They include the building of the canals, the areas where they were built, their effect upon the economy, and the reasons for canal decline, e.g. *In what ways did the development of canals benefit Britain in the late eighteenth and early nineteenth centuries? Why did the canal system nevertheless decline after 1840?* (Oxford, 1979). Some questions ask you for information about James Brindley.

There are three examples of questions analysed here: 'explain', 'describe and explain', and 'short notes'. You could easily adapt these plans to answer similar questions on other topics in Transport, e.g. *Describe the main improvements made to the roads of Britain in the period 1750 to 1820. Why was improvement necessary and what effects did it have?* (Southern, 1979) can be answered using the same approach as with the inland waterways question.

Specimen Question 1
What were the chief results for nineteenth-century Britain of the development of railways? (Southern, 1976)

The key words and phrases to note here are 'chief results', 'development', and 'nineteenth-century'. The question is asking you to show that you know how the spread of railways in Britain affected the country between 1801 and 1900. It might have been even clearer if it had started with the word 'explain'. The big danger to avoid is spending time on describing the building of particular lines, like the Liverpool and Manchester, or on technical developments, like the block signalling system. The examiner wants to read an account of the chief economic and social effects of the railways, so do not turn the question into an excuse for displaying your technical knowledge. You must also decide which results were the most important and devote most time to writing about them.

Suggested essay plan   *Introduction*   Railway age began in 1830: great expansion in 1840s. Built on much wider scale than canals; many advantages over both canals and stage coaches. By end of nineteenth century few people or places not affected.

1 Stimulated economic growth   a) *Industry*   i) Movement of goods, orders, etc. ii) Created huge demand for coal and iron. Railways became a separate industry in themselves. iii) Became an important export. British capital, knowledge and materials used throughout world.

b) *Agriculture*   i) Produce taken into towns: meat, milk, some cheese and butter, fruit, vegetables. ii) Fertilizers, machinery and animal feedstuffs carried to farmers: essential for 'High Farming'.

2 Urban growth   a) From 1830s great increase in movement from countryside into towns: mostly by rail. b) Spread of suburbs. c) Specific railway towns, e.g. Crewe.

3 Social effects   Growth of leisure for middle and working classes. Day excursions from 1840s (NB 6 million visited the Great Exhibition); longer seaside holidays from 1860s; rise of Blackpool, etc.

4 More efficient communications   Mail: first travelling sorting office 1838; penny post 1840; mail trains 1855; telegraph; national newspapers.

Conclusion   Most aspects of life affected. Influence on the economy crucial.

Specimen Question 2
Describe the main developments in inland water transport between 1760 and 1815. How did these developments help to promote change in industry during that period? (Oxford, 1976)

This question falls into the 'describe and explain' category. You are being asked for a description of inland water transport over 55 years, and an explanation of how this assisted industrial change. The wording does not ask you to say anything about the decline of canals, so make sure that you stick to the wording and the dates.

Suggested essay plan *Introduction* Moving bulky goods inland slow and expensive. Had been some river improvements before 1760.

1 The Brindley canals Include brief details of Brindley's vision of St. Andrew's cross. Include some of his canals, e.g. Trent and Mersey, Coventry, Oxford, etc. Contour canals, linking with navigable rivers where possible.

2 Canal mania and canals up to 1815 1790s: period of great investment, some schemes impractical. Canals which were built: more ambitious and therefore more expensive, e.g. Leeds and Liverpool. Therefore by 1815, main industrial and urban areas all linked; Birmingham centre of 'canal wheel'.

3 Industrial change a) Heavy, bulky goods could be carried long distances, e.g. coal, iron ore, grain, etc. b) Transport costs greatly reduced. c) Midlands area greatly benefited as did South Wales coalfield. Therefore, canals very important in the development of the Industrial and Agrarian revolutions.

Conclusion Canal/river system not finished by 1815. Vital to economic growth 1760–1815.

Specimen Question 3
State the main facts about four of the following and explain their importance in the development of roads and road transport in Britain. Metcalf; Trevithick; Palmer; London–Holyhead road; macadamisation; Sir G. Gurney. (Oxford, 1979)

You could easily come across this type of question in another topic, like railways, textiles, or social reform: it could be a selection of biographies and short topics, as here, or either on its own. One of the dangers to be aware of is writing too much, so you should try to spend roughly the same amount of time on each. Since there is thirty minutes for this question, you have about seven minutes for each of the four sections. Some of the information you need for the answer is in the chapter, although extra is included in the notes in some cases. It is likely that you will know least about macadamisation and Sir G. Gurney, so these have been left out.

Metcalf (1717–1810) Include details of his life; areas where he built roads; his methods.

Palmer In addition to what you will find in the chapter, it might also help you to know that he had suggested the idea of mail coaches in 1782, and that he was paid a pension of £3,000 a year from 1792 in recognition of his services.

London–Holyhead road Use the information in the chapter. Also note that the work involved two suspension bridges over the River Conwy and the Menai Straits. About 70 miles of the road followed Watling Street; it went through Birmingham and Daventry.

Trevithick (1771–1833) Early experience as mining engineer in Cornwall. Produced steam carriage called *Puffing Devil* in 1801; larger version driven to London in 1802, reaching 12 miles an hour. Patented high-pressure steam-engine 1802. 1804 locomotive at Penydarren Ironworks, near Merthyr Tydfil: pulled 5 coal wagons and 70 passengers, reaching 9 miles an hour. 1808 *Catch me who can* at Euston Square, London. Went off to South America. Died penniless. The real 'father of the steam locomotive'.

Chapter 5 *People, Poverty and Health*

This chapter is concerned with the rapid increase in population, its causes and some of its consequences, especially the problems of poverty in the early nineteenth century and public health in the rapidly expanding towns.

Population Growth 1750–1914

In 1750 there were about six million people in England and Wales. Because the first national census was not taken until 1801 this is only an approximate figure. However, from reasonably reliable estimates we know that while the population had grown relatively slowly before 1750, it rose more rapidly in the second half of the eighteenth century, especially from the 1770s. During the nineteenth century censuses were held every ten years and they record a population explosion as it doubled from 9 to 18 million between 1801 and 1851 and doubled again by 1911 when it reached 36 million. By then the total number of people in England and Wales had increased six times since 1750. The Scottish population had increased four times at the same time, rising from about 1.2 million in 1750 to 4.8 million in 1911. (In sharp contrast Ireland's population was little higher in the early twentieth century than it had been in the mid-eighteenth century. After doubling from 4 to 8 million between the 1780s and 1840s it then fell sharply.)

		Population (in millions) **England and Wales**			**Scotland**
	Population	**Countryside**	**London**	**Other towns**	**Population**
1750	6.0	4.7	0.6	0.7	1.2
1801	9.0	6.0	1.0	2.0	1.7
1851	18.0	9.0	2.7	6.3	2.9
1911	36.0	8.0	7.2	20.8	4.8

NB Figures for 1750 are approximate

Causes
It is very difficult to explain fully this population explosion which seems to have been caused both by people living longer and by an increase in the number of people born. Since births, deaths and marriages were not registered until 1838 we have inadequate information for the crucial earlier period. Historians used to believe that it was caused, in the later eighteenth century, by a decline in the death rate which was caused mainly by improved medical facilities, and preventing the drinking of cheap gin in 1751. More recently others have both successfully challenged these explanations and suggested that the rise in the birth rate may have been greater than the fall in the death rate.

The extent of the gin craze was greatly exaggerated by William Hogarth's famous cartoon and since it was mostly confined to London it had little overall effect on deaths in the whole country. However there were certainly important medical improvements from the eighteenth century. Advances in midwifery must have reduced the number of mothers and babies who died in child-birth. Smallpox was one of the main epidemic diseases which killed young people. The development of inoculation from the 1720s and then Edward Jenner's (1749–1823) technique of vaccination from 1796 both made significant contributions to reducing deaths from smallpox, but not until they were applied quite widely some time after they were introduced. (Vaccination was not made free until 1840.)

The hospitals that were founded in the eighteenth century (9 in London by 1760 and 38 in the provinces by 1800) were much less effective in making people healthier. Most were dirty and inefficient and important advances in hospitals did not occur until after 1847 with Simpson's anaesthetics, Joseph Lister's antiseptic surgery (1867) and Florence Nightingale's (1820–1910) nurses, followed by many other important developments.

Improved living standards may have contributed even more to making people live longer. Improvements in farming meant that more wheaten bread, meat and vegetables were produced. Transport developments reduced food prices and helped relieve temporary shortages. Better houses were built of brick with slated roofs which could be warmer and drier than previously, especially when heated by coal. Soap became more readily available. Cheap cotton clothing could be washed more easily than heavy woollen materials. Most of these improvements were enjoyed mainly by the upper and middle classes and in the countryside. The growth of large, crowded and insanitary areas in the towns in the early nineteenth century made the living conditions of some town dwellers worse.

From the figures that do exist we know that the **death-rate** in England and Wales was about 22 per 1,000 around 1840. Despite four major outbreaks of cholera between 1831 and 1866 and other epidemic diseases there were no long-term changes until the mid-1870s. Then the death rate began to fall steadily to about 14 per 1,000 around 1910. The **infant mortality rate** fell later. From 1840 to 1900 about 15 per cent of all children born died in their first year of life. By 1910 the rate had fallen to 11 per cent. Improvements in medicine combined with improved living conditions and standards of living account for this. In comparison we do not know when, by how much or why the death rate fell in the eighteenth century.

Between 1840 and the mid-1870s **the birth rate** rose from 32 per 1,000 of the population to 36, before starting to fall to 25 by 1910. After 1880 families got smaller as women started marrying later and contraceptive practices began to spread. The average number of children born to women who stayed married for 20 years or more fell from six, for those married in the 1860s, to four 30 years later.

Now it is quite likely that the birth rate began to rise in the eighteenth century. Almost certainly this was caused by couples marrying a few years earlier and having more children. Higher wages in industrial areas together with a decline in apprenticeship regulations, which prevented workers from marrying until a certain age, could have accounted in part for this. So could greater mobility, which enabled young couples to find a house to live in. A rising standard of living could also lead to a higher birth rate since healthier women conceive more often. But this is mere guessing. We only know that the birth rate rose in some areas and among some groups for part of the eighteenth century. But before 1840 we do not know for certain the national trend.

Migration

With more certainty we can say that the population explosion was not caused by the arrival of large numbers of people from other countries. During the later eighteenth and early nineteenth centuries some migrants came to England from Scotland and Ireland, especially in the later 1840s when a wave of stricken Irish immigrants tried to escape their famine- and disease-ridden country. But many English emigrated too, especially after the 1840s when steamships made cheaper long-distance travel to the colonies. Altogether England suffered a net loss by migration of 300,000 from 1851 to 1881, and of 1,200,000 between 1881 and 1911.

Reverend Thomas Malthus (1766–1834)

He was one of the first people to alert his contemporaries to the dangers of a rapidly rising population and to the need to take steps to limit it. In 1798 he published *An Essay on the Principle of Population* which made an immediate impact, was reprinted several times and constantly attacked. In it he argued that population tended to increase at a faster rate than its food supplies unless it was checked by poverty, epidemics, famine or people limiting their families. The controversy aroused by his essay was partly responsible for prompting the Government to accept John Rickman's idea of conducting a census, which he did in 1801. England's experience in the nineteenth century seemed to prove Malthus wrong. The massive growth of towns and changes in agriculture, transport and technology not only led to Britain feeding and housing the exploding population, but eventually to raising their standards of living too. And the increased population also played a vital role in stimulating the agricultural and industrial revolutions, with more mouths to feed, more people to work in the factories and more consumers to satisfy. But in Ireland Malthus's warnings materialized dreadfully in 1846 with a devastating famine.

Poor Law 1790–1850

By our standards most people in the eighteenth century were poor. But only those who were destitute and on the verge of starvation could hope for relief from the parish.

The old poor law which had developed during Elizabeth I's reign had been consolidated by the *Poor Law Act (1601)* and later strengthened by measures like the Act of Settlement (1662). Under this system each parish was responsible for its own poor. It appointed, annually, overseers of the poor to collect a compulsory Poor Rate (tax) from all householders and spend it on the very poor. Ideally the orphans should be educated, the unemployed given work and the sick and old provided with care and housing. The standards of relief varied considerably from one parish to the next. In practice most overseers gave weekly doles to the most unfortunate, paid for the lodging of some orphans and approved exceptional payments for funerals and fuel. To prevent some parishes from being flooded by paupers, the authorities could remove people back to the parish where they or their husbands had been born or apprenticed.

Finding work for the able-bodied was by far the most difficult task, made worse because the parishes were so small. Only a small minority contained more than 200 families. In 1723 Parliament allowed parishes to join together to build a workhouse, but the scheme failed. This failure was recognized by Gilbert's Act of 1782 which encouraged parishes to form unions to support a professional guardian to look after the impotent or non-able-bodied poor in 'workhouses' where nobody was now intended to work. Very few parishes took up this opportunity and the great majority of paupers continued to receive outdoor relief.

During the later eighteenth century the Old Poor Law failed to cope adequately with a great increase in poverty. The main reason was the continuing growth in population and shortage of employment especially in the countryside, but industrial change and wars also upset the economy. Then the price of food, which had been rising steadily, shot up in the 1790s because of bad harvests. Because labourers' wages did not rise as fast as prices many with families who still had work could no longer make both ends meet.

Speenhamland System
On 6 May 1795 twenty Berkshire magistrates considered the problem at the Pelican Inn in Speen, near Newbury. They decided to help the underpaid labourers by giving them an allowance in addition to their wages. This varied according to the price of bread so that (in theory) they could always buy 26 lbs (12 kg) of bread a week for themselves and 13 lbs (6 kg) for their wife and each dependent child. This method of supplementing wages was known as the Speenhamland System. Although it was not a national system it was adopted by many other counties in the south and Midlands, where sometimes the allowance was paid in flour.

In some parishes other methods were devised for helping unemployed labourers. By the **labour rate** ratepayers could choose either to pay their rates or to employ a certain number of paupers equivalent to the rates for which they were assessed. By the less popular **roundsman system** able-bodied pauper labourers were employed in turn by the farmer ratepayers in a parish. If their wages were inadequate the parish supplemented them. As with the Speenhamland System the farmers were naturally tempted to pay very low wages when they knew the parish would make them up. And the labourers had no chance of receiving any more however hard they worked because the level of their take-home pay depended on the allowances they received.

So many people needed help that the total spent on poor relief rose from £2 million in 1784 to £4 million in 1802 and £6 million in 1815. When allowance is made for rising population and inflation the increase was not so sharp, but contemporary ratepayers did not make these allowances, especially since the rates rose even higher between 1816 and 1820. As prices fell from 1813 some parishes abandoned the Speenhamland System and others paid allowances only for the third child or more in a family. Poverty and unemployment were greatest in the agricultural counties, especially those which specialized in growing wheat and they formed the great majority of those eighteen counties which were still operating the Speenhamland System in 1824.

As the burden of poor relief did not fall and the population rose rapidly, ratepayers were increasingly influenced by Malthus and his followers, who argued that the Speenhamland allowances were encouraging the farm labourers to breed and discouraging them from moving into the towns where there was work. (Recent research has shown that in most Speenhamland counties the population was rising at a lower rate than average, but at the time no one knew this.) A campaign to make the Poor Law harsher was helped in 1830 by a small increase in Poor Rates and widespread distress and disturbances in southern England (Swing riots).

The Poor Law Amendment Act (1834)

In *1832* a *Royal Commission* was set up to examine the working of the Poor Laws. *Edwin Chadwick* (1800–90) was its most influential member. Born in Manchester and trained as a barrister in London, he had become the friend and secretary of the Utilitarian philosopher Jeremy Bentham who, among many other things, wanted to encourage poor labourers to work by removing their right to poor relief. All the evidence presented to the commission favoured reducing rates and abolishing Speenhamland. Chadwick wanted relief to be given to the able-bodied only in workhouses which should be made so unpleasant that only those in real need would enter them. This was the central recommendation of their report in 1834 and Parliament accepted it immediately, along with most of the rest of the report.

To enforce the workhouse test the Poor Law Amendment Act grouped the parishes into *Unions*, each under a *Board of Guardians* elected by the ratepayers. To run the workhouses the Boards appointed full-time paid officials, who were supervised by the three Commissioners of the *Poor Law Commission*, with twelve Assistant Commissioners to exercise firm central control. Chadwick was bitterly disappointed not to be made one of these three Commissioners, but reluctantly he became the Commission's secretary.

The introduction of the New Poor Law took time, aroused bitter hostility and was never complete. Relief outside the workhouses continued, because it was more expensive to house paupers in well-regulated workhouses than to give them outdoor relief and most authorities were mainly concerned with keeping down rates. In 1840–5 only one pauper in seven received relief in a workhouse. By 1850 it was one pauper in eight. Most workhouses were clean and gave their inmates plain but sufficient food. However, they housed all different kinds of pauper and were very forbidding places. Strict rules separated men from women, forbade visitors, beer or tobacco and forced the able-bodied to work at tasks like stone-breaking. Some workhouses like Andover were appalling, and books like *Oliver Twist* by Charles Dickens have left the misleading impression that all were equally cruel.

Opposition and Changes

Despite many protests nearly all parishes in southern England were grouped into Unions by 1837 and the Commissioners started to apply the 1834 Act in the north. This coincided with one of the worst depressions in the nineteenth century, and for two years it met with bitter opposition from an organized *Anti-Poor Law Movement*. The policy which was designed to deal only with able-bodied unemployed in the countryside was totally inappropriate for the problems of industrial workers during a slump. The main causes of poverty in the towns were low earnings, irregular employment, large families, sickness, widowhood and old age, not laziness and drunkenness, and the New Poor Law provided no solution for them. Nor did it raise wages and improve living conditions as its supporters had predicted. Its insistence on making the mothers almost entirely responsible for supporting illegitimate children was also very harsh. However the cost of poor relief fell from £6 million in 1834 to £5 million in 1851. The unpopular Poor Law Commission was replaced in 1847 by a *Poor Law Board*, but the principles of 1834 survived as the basis of poor relief until the early twentieth century. Although some of the harshest aspects of the workhouses were eventually modified, dread of ending their days in a workhouse was the most common fear of all the Victorian working classes.

Older historians have tended to accept, without question, the most extreme accounts of the failings of the Old Poor Law and of the new workhouses. Recent research has shown that the truth is only partly contained within this propaganda of both the 1834 Poor Law Report and the Anti-Poor Law Movement.

Public Health in Towns 1815–1914

The population explosion could not have continued throughout the nineteenth century without an even more *rapid growth of towns*. The numbers living in towns in England and Wales rose from 3 million in 1801 to 28 million by 1911 and the proportion from one-third in 1801 to a half in 1851 and over three-quarters in 1911. This urban growth had started long before 1801. In the second half of the eighteenth century the urban population had doubled, while in Manchester alone it had quadrupled at least. But apart from London eighteenth-century towns were all small in comparison with the later period. Before 1780 London and Edinburgh were the only two towns in Britain with more than 50,000 inhabitants. By 1900 there were eighty more and some of these had merged into others to form even bigger conurbations. Most of these big towns were located where industry had grown on or near the coalfields of the Midlands, Lancashire, the West Riding of Yorkshire, the North-east, South Wales and Central Scotland.

Hazards to Health
Because most people walked wherever they went, thousands of rows of terraced houses were built as near as possible to the centre of towns. And because working men could rarely afford to pay more rent than two shillings per week, most were built as cheaply as possible (perhaps £50 each) and often back-to-back. By the mid-nineteenth century, therefore, working-class homes not only lacked kitchens, lavatories and bathrooms, but were often damp, draughty, overcrowded and dirty too. Normally several families shared one outdoor privy. These drained into cess-pits which often leaked and were not emptied regularly. Many families could only get rid of their refuse and excrement by dumping it in the nearby streets which were infrequently cleaned and rarely paved and lit. (Only the main streets and those in the wealthier quarters were in better condition.) Water had to be fetched from wells and streams, or else private water companies piped it in from rivers. All these sources could easily become contaminated. Other hazards to health in crowded towns were overstocked graveyards, the obnoxious waste from some factories and tanneries and the smoke which heavily polluted the air over most towns in winter.

In the early nineteenth century the local town councils were entirely responsible for their own conditions. Few took any effective action because improvements were expensive and the wealthy rarely saw the homes of the poorer workers. Only after determined campaigning by men like Chadwick was the situation changed.

Edwin Chadwick (1800–90)
Chadwick's work for the Poor Law Commission brought home to him the close connection between poverty and illness. He soon realized that if only towns were made cleaner, people would become both healthier and less poor, but the Poor Rate could not be spent on public health. The Commissioners report for 1838 contained telling sections which showed that many widows and orphans in London

were receiving poor relief simply because their husbands or fathers had died of fevers, like typhus, whose germs spread in filthy conditions. Much of it was based on the work of three doctors, **Arnott, Kay** who had published in 1832 an account of conditions in Manchester, and **Southwood Smith** of the London Fever Hospital. Chadwick also made good use of the registration of deaths from 1838 to show how much healthier country people were than town-dwellers.

Prompted by Chadwick, a survey of the whole country was begun in 1839, but because of opposition it was not completed until **1842**. Then the **Report on the Sanitary Condition of the Labouring Population** was published under Chadwick's own name. His vivid descriptions and telling statistics shocked an ignorant public into learning how bad much of the towns really were. (In 1840 for instance, the average age of death for labourers and their families in Liverpool was 15 and in Rutland 38). The report also showed how wrong it was to blame these filthy conditions only on the personal failings of the poor. Chadwick recommended that the towns should dispose of their sewage through a network of narrow drain-pipes made of glazed pottery, that the local authorities should provide all houses with a water supply and that medical officers should get conditions at work improved. In 1843 he published another report exposing the shocking conditions of many graveyards and recommending that cemeteries be set up on the outskirts of towns.

Government Reaction

Uncertain what to do, the government in **1843** set up a **Royal Commission on the Health of Towns**, which confirmed Chadwick's findings in 1844. Out of fifty towns investigated, only one had reasonable drainage and only six had good water supplies. In 1845 it recommended the creation of a strong Central Board of Health. It was set up at last by the **Public Health Act** in **1848**, with limited powers and only for a five year period, with Chadwick as a member. It could only set up local boards of health where 10 per cent of the ratepayers requested one, or where the death rate exceeded 23 per 1,000 (i.e. above the national average). The return of cholera in 1848–9, killing 53,000, frightened some areas into improving their water supplies, drainage and streets. Further progress was delayed by cost and by serious disagreements between doctors over the causes of some diseases, and between engineers over methods of drainage. Chadwick was an impatient man who made many enemies as he tried to persuade councils to act. His opponents got the Board of Health disbanded in 1854 and replaced by one with weaker powers for four years. Chadwick was given a pension of £1,000 per year, but not another job.

Progress was slow after 1854. Not until cholera threatened again in **1866** was the **Sanitary Act** passed requiring local authorities to act over water supplies and the disposal of sewage and waste. But the local boards needed central guidance which was partly given to them from 1871 by the Local Government Board which had as its chief medical officer, **John Simon** (1816–1904) who had been London's first Medical Officer of Health from 1848 to 1855 and the principal adviser to the government on public health since 1858.

By **1875** there were so many different and complicated public health laws that Disraeli's government passed the **Public Health Act** to bring them all together. It also created a uniform system of sanitary authorities throughout the country consisting of the Town Councils and, in the countryside, Poor-Law Unions. All had to appoint medical officers of health and sanitary inspectors. In the later nineteenth century they became more effective with better training, wider powers as, for example, the notification of infectious diseases, and improved knowledge about the germs of tuberculosis, cholera, typhoid, etc. But still John Simon was dissatisfied with the very limited powers of the Local Government Board to force the pace and in 1876 he resigned. A Ministry of Health was not created until 1919.

Later Developments

It took at least another generation of great endeavour before **adequate water supplies** were fully available, and the working classes could regularly use water closets and wash in warm water and soap. At the same time deaths from most infectious diseases fell sharply, but it took far longer for **housing** to be improved. By the Torrens Act of 1868 local authorities were given the power to demolish or repair single houses in an unsanitary condition. The Artisans' Dwellings Act (1875) gave them much wider powers to pull down whole slum areas. But, since the authorities had to pay compensation and rehouse those dispossessed, only limited use was made of this Act by a few towns like Birmingham. These Acts were strengthened in 1879 and 1882 but still a Royal Commission on the Housing of the Working Class (1884–5) revealed how widespread bad housing was. The Commission produced no overall solution, but a major Housing Act was passed in 1890. It simplified and strengthened the earlier laws and encouraged authorities to engage in improvement schemes and build houses, but like the earlier laws it did not compel them and most ignored it. Although high standards were laid down for by-laws for new housing, the building of back-to-back houses was not finally prohibited until 1909. Because the towns continued to expand so rapidly, bad housing was one of the major legacies acquired by the twentieth century from the Victorians, and it took a long time to resolve. Laws alone could not bring about improvements in urban conditions.

Statistics

Growth of selected towns: population
(in thousands)

	1801	1851	1911
Birmingham	71	215	840
Bradford	13	104	288
Bristol	61	137	357
Glasgow	77	375	1,000
Leeds	53	172	453
Liverpool	82	395	746
Manchester	75	340	714
Salford	14	64	231
Sheffield	46	135	455

Population of conurbations in 1901
(in millions)

London	6.5
S.E. Lancashire	2.1
W. Midlands	1.5
W. Yorkshire	1.5
Clydeside	1.3
Merseyside	1.0
Tyneside	0.7
	14.6

However, though progress was slow, and few people believed that poverty, disease and poor housing could be eliminated by government action, the idea that the State had a responsibility to protect the lives of its citizens did gain ground during the last quarter of the nineteenth century. This was a remarkable shift from the philosophy which gave birth to the New Poor Law.

Guide to Questions

The questions on these topics will vary a great deal, but do try to answer them as clearly as possible, including accurate factual information, since essays can include brief generalizations which might suggest that you only have a vague idea what you are writing about. Most of the questions on population growth are of the 'explain' variety, and cover the period 1760–1914, although most deal with the nineteenth century. Usually, you will be asked for the reasons for population growth, and its consequences; sometimes, you have to include details on the distribution of the population as well. Some of the questions do involve statistics.

The questions on towns and public health are mainly 'describe', and can cover all of the nineteenth century and up to 1914, but usually they deal with either the first or second halves of the century. Normally, you are asked to explain why towns grew so rapidly, and to describe improvements in urban conditions, e.g. *Why did some towns grow so rapidly in the first half of the nineteenth century? What problems were caused by this growth?* (Southern, 1976), and *What steps were taken during the nineteenth century to make English cities healthier to live in? Illustrate your answer with examples from particular areas if you can* (Oxford, 1977). Some of the questions do expect a knowledge of the main Public Health Acts.

Most of the questions dealing with poverty are 'describe' or 'describe and explain'. Almost all concentrate on the Poor Law Amendment Act of 1834, and expect you to know about the previous methods of poor relief, why the 1834 Act was passed, and what its consequences were. Some of the questions might include stimulus material, like documents.

Specimen Question 1
What reasons are said to explain the increase in the population of Great Britain between 1801 and 1851? (Southern, 1978).

This is still a controversial topic amongst historians, and many of the text books do not tell you this. The examiners have worded this question very carefully, but they do not always do so. You should show that you are aware that information on population is in short supply before 1838, and that the early census figures are not entirely reliable.

The question falls into the 'explain' category, and it is likely that a fair amount of your essay will be spent explaining why medical changes, a lower death rate, migration, etc., cannot explain the nineteenth-century population explosion. Beware of including details after 1851, e.g. Florence Nightingale or Lister: the examiners are very clear here on the period they want you to write about.

Suggested essay plan *Introduction* Census every ten years from 1801. Population increased from 9 to 18 million 1801–51: start of population explosion; historians still uncertain about reasons.

1 Death rate Used to be thought that a decline in death rate was main explanation.

1840 figure about 22 per 1,000: seems to remain constant for next 30 years, but before 1840: guesswork. Infant mortality high: about 15 per cent. So, not possible to use death rate to explain population explosion 1801–51.

2 Birth rate It does seem after 1838 more people being born and that up to 1870s a rising birth rate: probably from late eighteenth century. People marrying earlier; higher standard of living, so couples having children earlier. Yet, much guesswork: it varied from area to area: evidence 1801–51 scanty.

3 Living standards There were the following improvements: a) farming: more meat, bread, vegetables; b) better transport: foodstuffs more available; c) better housing: bricks, slate; warmer, drier; heated by coal; d) cleanliness: soap; cotton clothes. But these were offset by the rapid growth of towns.

4 Medical improvements a) Had been some before 1801, e.g. midwifery and smallpox; but Jenner's vaccination not free until 1840. b) Hospitals: in London and provinces. Most were dirty and inefficient.

5 Migration Population increase 1801–51 not caused by large-scale immigration. There were immigrants, largely from Scotland and Ireland (NB the effects of the Irish famine) but many English left too, especially after the 1840s.

Conclusion Little reliable evidence 1801–51. Conclusions only intelligent guesswork.

Specimen Question 2

Show the contribution made by four of the following to the improvement of living conditions in Britain: Cadbury, Chadwick, J. Chamberlain, Disraeli, Octavia Hill, Sir John Simon, Southwood Smith (Oxford, 1978).

A 'short notes' question about seven nineteenth-century reformers. The notes have left out Cadbury, Chamberlain and Disraeli, and include information not to be found in the chapter. Try to spend a similar amount of time on each of the four, and, if you were to choose Chamberlain and Disraeli in the examination, beware of writing an answer on their political careers in general.

Edwin Chadwick (1800–90) Use the information in the chapter to show his wide interests in social reform, including public health, housing, burials, etc. He was a leading nineteenth-century reformer, but was forced into early retirement in 1854. Was knighted in 1889.

Octavia Hill (1832–1912) Shocked by poverty in London: devoted her life to helping poor, especially by housing schemes. Leased houses to poor families, trained people to manage these lodging houses. Established clubs: early community centres. Advocated playgrounds for children and open spaces. Started the National Trust; member of the 1905 Royal Commission on Poor Laws.

Sir John Simon (1816–1904) Doctor and health administrator. 1848: Medical Officer of Health for London: for seven years. Issued annual reports, produced local statistics. 1855: first medical officer of General Board of Health; 1858 of Health Department of Privy Council; 1871 of the Local Government Board. Retired 1876. Laid basis for future administration of health in towns.

Thomas Southwood Smith (1788–1861) Doctor, sanitary reformer, Evangelical. 1824: physician at London Fever Hospital: published *Treatise on Fever* in 1830. Took part in inquiry into factory children in 1833, and 1834 inquiry for Poor Law Commission. 1839: main founder of Health of Towns Association. 1848: Board of Health.

Specimen Question 3

Why was the Poor Law Amendment Act passed in 1834? Describe the changes it made in the organization and provision of poor relief (Cambridge, 1979).

This is a structured question, with three parts: the reasons for the Act of 1834, the organization of poor relief, and the new provisions: so the wording of the question provides a basic essay plan. This kind of question expects you to know something about the Old Poor Law—dating from the reigns of Elizabeth I and Charles II—and the Speenhamland System. Make sure that you point out that poor relief did vary from area to area, and that there was no national system until after 1834.

Suggested essay plan   *Introduction*   Most Poor Law relief dated from the seventeenth century. Speenhamland System from the 1790s.

1 Attack on the Old Poor Law   Strong anti-Poor Law propaganda after about 1818 by Utilitarians and others: pointed to increased costs, and views of Malthus. Events of 1830 brought this campaign to a head.

2 Royal Commission   Set up 1832. Benthamites very influential: believed that poor should be encouraged to work: the Report reflected their views. There should be a national system; Speenhamland abolished; workhouses. Most of these recommendations in Act of 1834.

3 The New Poor Law   Parishes grouped into Unions, each with Board of Guardians elected by ratepayers. Board appointed officials to run workhouses; whole system supervised by Central Board: Chadwick as secretary. Workhouses based on 'less eligibility': not intended to be cruel, but to deter lazy.

4 The system in operation   Took time, never complete; outside relief still continued: to keep down rates. 1837: most southern English parishes grouped; system began to operate in north: bitter opposition: coincided with severe depression, and new system not designed to cope with it. System remained in operation until twentieth century.

Conclusion   Old methods brought into disrepute by 1834. The New Poor Law: first national system, but did vary from place to place: outdoor relief still paid.

Chapter 6 *Trade Unions to 1927*

Today we assume that all workers should be able to protect their interests by joining recognized trade unions. No one assumed this in the early nineteenth century. Then trade unions were bitterly opposed by most employers and the government. Parliament also took no responsibility for protecting workmen against illness or unemployment or for regulating their hours or conditions of work. The struggle to change this was long, bitter and complex. As late as the 1880s only one adult male manual-worker in ten was protected by a trade union. Then trade union membership rose rapidly: 0.75 million in 1888; 1.5 million in 1891; 2 million in 1900; 2.5 million in 1910; 4 million in 1914; 8 million in 1919.

Background to 1825

The **earliest unions** developed in the eighteenth century as 'trade clubs' or societies among skilled (apprenticed) craftsmen in particular trades, like printing and shoe-making. Most were very small and local, concerned mainly with beating off the threat of unemployment and helping their least fortunate members. Some of the most successful negotiated agreed wage rates with all the masters in their town. Strikes and violence were usually adopted only as a last resort by the less well-organized, like hand-loom weavers.

Most trade union activities were already illegal when fear of French revolutionary ideas spreading drove Parliament to pass new **Combination Acts** in 1799 and 1800. These made it easier to prosecute workmen who combined over their wages or hours. In practice they were not enforced widely, but their threat remained. During the early nineteenth century unions even spread in the cotton industry. In Lancashire the mule-spinners engaged in two major strikes in 1810 and 1818.

Long after the French wars were over and the government's attitude had changed, a London tailor, Francis Place (1771–1854), campaigned successfully to persuade Parliament to **repeal** the Combination Acts in 1824. Because trade was booming and the employers could afford to pay higher wages, this triggered off so many strikes and trade union demands that Parliament revised the law in 1825. Workmen could now form trade unions and bargain over wages and hours, but not over apprentices nor could they 'molest or obstruct' persons at work. Trade unions could operate openly without fear, but many laws still survived against them.

Expansion 1825–34

Trade unions expanded in the later 1820s. In 1826 the Friendly Union of Mechanics was founded in Manchester, in 1827 a General Union of Bricklayers and Carpenters was set up and in 1829 John Doherty formed a Grand General Union of Operative Spinners from his Manchester Cotton Spinners Union. Miners, potters and printers also organized wider unions. Then Doherty's attempt to establish the National Association for the Protection of Labour for all trades in 1830 soon foundered.

The Grand National Consolidated Trade Union (GNCTU)
This was formed in 1833 to support trade unionists in Derby against their employers. It was strongly influenced by **Robert Owen** who believed that workers would only be rewarded better if society was changed. After failing to establish co-operative communities in America, Owen had encouraged co-operative societies in Britain. Then he produced a draft plan for a general union for all workers in October 1833.

At first the GNCTU was well supported, especially by the London tailors and shoemakers, but it never had 500,000 members as was once thought. Only 16,000 paid their subscriptions. The growth of unionism worried the government, especially in the countryside. In February 1834 when the GNCTU was launched officially, George Loveless and five other farm labourers from **Tolpuddle** in Dorset were arrested. In March they were found guilty of administering illegal oaths to recruits for their union and were transported to Australia for seven years. A big campaign to get these Tolpuddle martyrs released did not succeed until 1836.

The **GNCTU soon collapsed**. Most working men were too poor, too illiterate, too frightened by the fate of the Tolpuddle six, and too unconcerned with workers from other trades to support a national general union. The GNCTU could not protect its supporters from threats by many employers to dismiss them if they did not sign a Document stating that they neither belonged to, nor intended to join, a union. In August 1834 its president, Owen, dissolved the GNCTU officially.

Developments 1835–75

From 1835 trade unions *grew steadily in the traditional pattern* of skilled workers from one trade in one locality. They flourished best in trades like printing that were little affected by industrial developments and in industries, like textiles, coal-mining and engineering, that were affected most. In textiles there were separate unions for different regions and processes such as spinning and weaving. Coal-mining expanded rapidly in the 1840s and had separate unions in each coalfield. Both industries relied on Parliament to improve their working conditions although their wages were negotiated locally.

The Amalgamated Society of Engineers
The engineering unions responded differently to the growth of new machines and factories. In 1838 the Journeymen Steam-Engine Makers' Society (JSEMS) was formed from the Mechanics' unions of Manchester and Yorkshire. It appointed a full-time secretary in 1845 and opposed the employers vigorously. They knew they would be stronger if all the engineering unions joined together and so, in 1851, formed the Amalgamated Society of Engineers, Machinists, Smiths, Millwrights and Pattern-makers (ASE).

The ASE was based on the JSEMS, whose secretary, **William Allan**, moved to its new headquarters in London. In less than a year it had almost 12,000 skilled members paying the high weekly subscription of one shilling and eligible for generous financial benefits when they were in trouble. In 1852 the ASE entered a bitter struggle with the employers, against piecework and overtime, which it lost. It took several years for the ASE to be recognized by the employers and for its numbers to revive. By the 1860s its policy was to avoid strikes if possible. The ASE is often described as a **new model union**, but it was much more the end of the development of the **traditional craft unions** than a new departure. It also served only as a model to the ironfounders and the unions in the building trades.

The London building unions' demand for their working day to be cut from ten to nine hours led to a winter of strikes and lock-outs in 1859–60. A gift of £3,000 from the ASE helped save the building workers from defeat. The Carpenters and Joiners immediately formed their own Amalgamated Society and made the very able 28 year-old, **Robert Applegarth** their secretary in 1862. Soon afterwards the bricklayers and plasterers reorganized themselves on similar lines, with a full-time secretary, a London headquarters, local branches and a policy favouring friendly society benefits rather than confrontation. But no union rivalled the size or wealth of the ASE, which had 45,000 members by 1880.

Opposition
Few other unions copied this model. In both London and the provinces many regarded them as smug and out of touch with the real concerns of the ordinary working man. In the **Sheffield cutlery trades**, for instance, the various unions' attempts to win concessions from the masters had been thwarted constantly by the encouragement or introduction of non-union workmen. In desperation the unionists had resorted to petty acts of violence, which culminated in one man's house being blown up in 1866. Public opinion was so shocked that a **Royal Commission** was appointed in **1867** to investigate these Sheffield outrages and trade unions generally.

In the same year (1867), the unions were threatened by the judgement in the case of **Hornby v Close** which ruled that the Boilermakers' Society could not recover £24 from its Bradford secretary. The judges argued that because unions acted 'in restraint of trade' they did not exist legally and so could not sue in the courts.

During the 1860s **trades councils**, with representatives from many different unions, had been formed in London and the other major cities. **The Reform Act of 1867**, which gave the vote to many working men for the first time, helped them defeat this double threat to the existence of trade unions. The London Trades Council was dominated by Applegarth, Allan and three other secretaries of national unions who were known as the Clique, but were later called the **Junta**. They persuaded the Royal Commission that the Sheffield cutlers' behaviour was quite exceptional and that most unions were co-operative and should be given greater legal protection.

Trades Union Congress
During this crisis thirty-four delegates had attended the first Trades Union Congress (TUC) at Manchester in 1868, called by George Potter and other opponents of the Junta to discuss matters of common concern to the unions. At the TUC's next meetings in Birmingham (1869) and London (1871), representatives from the London Trades Council were present and they concentrated on trying to influence the new laws that Parliament was considering. When the TUC set up a permanent Parliamentary Committee in 1871 the unions were at last fully organized on a national basis.

Changes in the Law

The Trade Union Act (1871) gave the unions legal recognition and protected their funds from dishonest officials, but the *Criminal Law Amendment Act (1871)* prevented their members from picketing to try to persuade others to join a strike. After much lobbying by the TUC's Parliamentary Committee, Disraeli's Conservative government passed the *Conspiracy and Protection of Property Act (1875)* which permitted peaceful picketing during a strike. The *Employers and Workmen Act (1875)* removed another longstanding trade-union grievance. Workmen who broke a contract would now be fined and not imprisoned, like the employers.

Growth of Unions

In the trade boom of the early 1870s trade unions were formed by some semi-skilled workers and labourers who had not been organized permanently before. Some were short-lived, like the gasworkers and builders' labourers in London. The *Amalgamated Society of Railway Servants* (1871) survived. At first it favoured arbitration rather than strikes.

The National Agricultural Labourers Union (NALU) was founded in 1872 by a Warwickshire methodist preacher, Joseph Arch. It reached a peak of nearly 1,000 branches and 86,000 members in 1874, but when the farmers' counter-attack was combined with the agricultural depression, the NALU soon began to crumble and was finally dissolved in 1896.

Trade Unions and Socialism 1875–1914

The depression that affected trade and industry from 1874 was not as severe or continuous as in agriculture. There were periods of prosperity around 1883 and 1890. *Prices fell* by 40 per cent by the mid-1890s, but they recovered to 85 per cent of the 1874 level by 1914. Since this rise in prices coincided with more *intense competition* from Britain's industrial rivals, many employers resisted wage claims to keep up with inflation.

New Unionism

After many unions advanced steadily in the early 1880s, there was a quite exceptional burst of trade union activity in the boom of 1889–91, when the number of trade union members doubled. This revival was heralded by several well-publicized and successful strikes, mainly in London. In 1888 Mrs Annie Besant helped the match-girl workers of Bryant and May to win more pay and better conditions.

In March 1889 Will Thorne, a young Birmingham-born Irishman who could barely read or write, began to organize a union at the Beckton Gas Works, East Ham, helped by Karl Marx's daughter, Eleanor. Within four months their *Gas Workers' and General Labourers' Union* had 20,000 members. When they threatened to strike, the South Metropolitan Gas Company and many others cut the stokers' working day from 12 to 8 hours.

These victories inspired *Ben Tillett* (1860–1943), the secretary of a Tea Warehousemen's union formed in 1887, to lead a strike of his fellow dockers at the West India Dock in August 1889. Since most dockers were casual labourers who were employed, for low wages, only when there was work, they demanded to be taken on for at least four hours at a time and to be paid a minimum of sixpence an hour (the dockers' tanner) and eightpence for overtime. Within a few days most of London's dockers supported them and the whole port was closed.

To run the strike, a committee was hastily organized. Every day John Burns led a huge procession of orderly but determined dockers through the streets of London. By arousing public sympathy they received many contributions, including £30,000 from Australia. After five weeks the Lord Mayor of London and Cardinal Manning persuaded the employers to grant the dockers' main demands. The new **Dockers' Union** had 40,000 members by 1890, with Tom Mann as president and Ben Tillett as secretary.

Other new unions were soon formed, including one for seamen and the **General Railway Workers' Union** for casual railway labourers. At last the miners were brought together in the **Miners Federation of Great Britain** (1889) and even the ASE agreed in 1892 to include some semi-skilled workers. For a short time these new unions brought a new impetus to the development of trade unions. They adopted a much more aggressive attitude to the employers. They were not concerned with friendly benefits but **improving pay and conditions**. Many of their leaders were Socialists with a much wider outlook than simply promoting the sectional interests of their members. They were the first to show concern for women workers. Their attempts to recruit general labourers both within and outside their industry were helped by cheaper travel and more schooling.

Opposition
Another recession from 1892 changed all this. With profits falling, the employers fought back. The gasworkers had already lost over half their members by 1892 and the Dockers' Union fell to 10,000 by 1910. The 'new unions' provided only one trade unionist in ten by the early twentieth century and to survive had adopted policies more like the older unions.

The employers counter-attacked against the unions. They formed their own federations in Shipping, Engineering, etc. and used organizations like the **National Free Labour Association** (1893) to break many strikes of the less skilled with non-union labourers. In 1893 strikes in cotton spinning and the Hull docks ended in compromise, but the miners won their lock-out. The ASE suffered the worst defeat in 1897. Their demand for an 8-hour day was answered by a national lock-out. After six months the ASE gave in, when it was also forced to accept piecework.

The judges supported this counter-attack. They ruled that picketing was illegal during a strike, even without the threat of violence, in the case of **Lyons v Wilkins** (1896). In 1900 the **Taff Vale Railway Co.** used non-union labour to defeat a strike for more wages and union recognition by the Amalgamated Society of Railway Servants (ASRS). Worse followed when this Welsh company sued the ASRS for damages suffered during the strike. In 1901 the award of £23,000 was upheld by the House of Lords and threatened all unions. **The Trade Disputes Act** of 1906 at last reversed these decisions and restored the legal immunity of trade unions.

The Labour Party
The thirty Labour MPs elected to Parliament in 1906 had strongly influenced the new Liberal government. The Labour Representation Committee, founded in 1900 by some trade unions and socialists, had grown rapidly into the Labour Party. It had one million members by 1906. The party's funds came mainly from a small political

levy paid by the members of unions affiliated to it. In a case brought by **W. V. Osborne**, a London official of the ASRS, the House of Lords ruled in 1909 that the union could not raise the levy from its members. The blow was softened in 1911 when MPs were paid £400 a year. In 1913 the **Trade Union Act** brought back the political levy, but let individuals refuse to pay it.

Renewed Activity

In **1910–14** there was renewed union expansion and bitter industrial conflict. In 1910 Mann and Tillett formed the **National Transport Workers Federation**, which secured wage increases for the dockers and seamen in 1911, but failed in another strike in 1912 to stop the Port of London from employing non-unionists. After a two-day national railway stoppage in 1911, the railway companies at last recognized the rail unions. In 1913 three of them merged into the **National Union of Railwaymen**, but the engine drivers and clerks remained separate.

In 1912 a national coal strike brought out a million miners for six weeks. They failed to obtain a minimum wage of five shillings per shift throughout the country, but different minimum wages were agreed in each district. Rising prices and full employment were the main causes of this renewed militancy. As the unions grew bigger, some leaders also believed they were engaged in a class war against the employers. Representatives of the miners, railwaymen and transport workers agreed in 1914 on the advantages of a **triple alliance** representing 1½ million men.

Industrial Conflict 1914–27

The number of trade unionists rose from 4 million in 1914 to 8 million in 1919–20. It then declined to 5.5 million in 1922–5 and 5 million by 1927. In 1920 one working man in two belonged to a union and one woman in four. By 1927 these proportions had fallen to 1 in 3 and 1 in 8. The general unions were affected most by these fluctuations.

First World War (1914–18)

Although the employers and unions agreed on an industrial truce during the war, there were some unofficial strikes notably among shipbuilders on Clydeside, miners in South Wales and police in London. But most unions co-operated with employers and the government. They emerged from the war with greatly increased funds, twice as many members, some improvements in working conditions, a better accepted role in industry and many potential grievances.

Post-war Problems

The scene was set for bitter battles. During the war the government had controlled the mines and railways and the unions did not want them handed back to their private owners. In industries like engineering, women and some unqualified men had replaced those who had gone to fight and the unions would not accept such dilution in peacetime. Millions of demobilized soldiers and sailors also expected to get back their old jobs. Until 1920 the post-war boom eased the situation. However, the cost of living went on rising but many men's wages did not keep up. After the boom broke in 1920, rapidly falling prices led the employers to press for lower wages and longer hours. These were bitterly resented, but the rapidly increasing unemployment weakened the ability of most unions to resist.

Strikes
An average of 16 million days a year had been lost through strikes in 1910–14. After the war the total rose to 35 million in 1919, 26.5 million in 1920 and 86 million in 1921, before declining to 20 million in 1922 and 10.5 million in 1923. These strikes covered many issues and affected many trades and industries, including the cotton operatives (1919 and 1921), ironfounders (1919), engineers (1922), shipyard workers (1922) and boilermakers (1923). However the principal strikes concerned the mines, railways and docks as in the years before the war.

Lloyd George's government avoided a strike in the coal mines in 1919, by setting up a Royal Commission, under *Sir John Sankey*, to look at a wide range of problems. Eventually the government rejected the Commission's recommendation to keep the mines nationalized and built up further trouble. In the meanwhile it tried to force lower wages on the railway workers, who held a national strike in September 1919 and made the government back down. In 1920 the London dockers won wage increases, without striking, from an industrial court where *Ernest Bevin* skilfully put their case.

In April 1921 the mines were returned to the coal owners who immediately proposed heavy cuts in wages. The miners rejected them and were locked out. A fortnight later the railwaymen and transport workers withdrew their promised sympathetic strike at the last minute on 'Black Friday'. After three months the miners surrendered and accepted huge wage cuts.

Amalgamations
In this period of weakness some workers tried to gain strength by forming bigger unions. In 1921 several unions joined the ASE to create the *Amalgamated Engineering Union*. In 1922 the *Transport and General Workers Union* (TGWU) was formed from the dockers' and carters' unions with Bevin as secretary. The *National Union of General and Municipal Workers* emerged in 1924 from another merger including Will Thorne's Gasworkers. In 1924 37 per cent of all trade unionists belonged to the six biggest unions.

The price of coal fell again in 1925 when the government returned to the Gold Standard. The coal owners proposed more wage cuts and this time the railwaymen and TGWU supported the miners. Baldwin's government kept up their wages with a subsidy and set up the *Samuel Commission* to review the situation. In 1926 it recommended wage cuts which the Miners' Federation rejected. The TUC General Council, successor to the Parliamentary Committee, prepared to support them when the subsidy ran out.

The General Strike
This began on 4 May 1926. All transport, electricity and gas workers, printers, iron, steel and chemical workers struck in support of the miners. Nearly 3 million men came out from those jobs most likely to paralyse the country. The government had planned carefully for this for nearly a year. Troops were sent to the docks and power stations and to protect food convoys into the towns. Volunteers drove buses and trains, acted as special constables and printed the government's newspaper '*The British Gazette*'. The TUC replied with '*The British Worker*'. Violent incidents were rare.

After a week the strike seemed to be going well for the unions, but the TUC leaders lost their nerve. Fearing that it might turn into an attack on the government, they started negotiations and suddenly called off the strike on 12 May. They had won no concessions for the miners who struggled on alone bitterly for six months before accepting defeat.

In 1927 the government forced through Parliament the **Trade Disputes Act** which made illegal most kinds of sympathetic strike and the Labour Party's political levy, unless union members asked to pay it. Outwardly the trade union movement's fortunes were at a very low ebb. However, most members remained loyal to their unions and the TUC, which had shown conclusively that its intentions were not revolutionary, was well placed to give effective leadership in the future.

Guide to Questions

Questions on trade unions are normally set on the whole period covered by this chapter. There is a strong tendency for those from the nineteenth century to be either descriptive or 'describe and explain' essays. *What were the most important landmarks in the history of the trade unions between 1830 and 1880?* (Southern, 1977) and *Give an account of the principal developments and changes in trade unionism between 1868 and 1914.* (London, 1980) are two reliable examples of descriptive essays.

Why, and in what ways, was the trade union movement more powerful in 1914 than it had been in 1870? (Oxford, 1979 and 1980) is clearly a popular 'describe and explain' essay with one board. Another one is: *Describe and explain the development of trade unions between 1815 and 1875.* (JMB, 1979).

More structured essays are set on the General Strike and the early twentieth century. For example: *Give an account of the main causes, events and results of the General Strike. Do you think the General Strike was justified or not? Give reasons for your answer.* (AEB, 1979).

If your board sets imaginary or stimulus questions, they are more likely to be on this later period.

Finally, two very different questions set by the same board will be considered in more detail.

Specimen Question 1

What were the most important landmarks in the history of trade unions between 1830 and 1880? (Southern, 1977).

This is a relatively straightforward descriptive essay. However, it does depend on you being able to identify the most important landmarks. You must also confine your essay to the fifty-year period covered by the question.

Suggested essay plan   *Introduction*   The legal position of the trade unions after 1825.

1 **Tolpuddle martyrs (1834)**   Trade union expansion of late 1820s and early 1830s (including GNCTU) halted decisively by action by the government and the employers (the Document).

2 **ASE (1851)**   Unions for skilled workers continued to develop. Engineers strongest in 1850s and model for some other building workers in 1860s.

3 **Legal changes**   Royal Commission (1867–9) sympathetic to trade unions despite

Sheffield outrages and *Hornby v Close*—success for Junta. 1871 trade unions got legal recognition and funds protected. 1875 peaceful picketing and equality at law for workmen with employers.

4 *TUC (1868)* Unions at last began to join together effectively after threat from Royal Commission and *Hornby v Close*. Set up Parliamentary Committee 1871.

Conclusion Continuing struggle by trade unions for improved legal status and expansion. Only a small minority of workers still belonged to trade unions in 1880.

Specimen Question 2

Why were there so many strikes and threats of strikes in the period 1918 to 1926? (Southern, 1979).

This explanatory question is much more difficult. You must avoid turning it into an essay on the causes of the General Strike or a description of industrial unrest between 1918 and 1926. Of course both are connected with this essay, but the question is asking why there were so many strikes and threats of strikes in this eight-year period and you must tackle this one.

Certainly you will have to indicate briefly which workers were most involved in industrial unrest, but the main part of the essay should be about Britain's economic problems after 1918 and the ways in which people's behaviour made the situation worse.

The material for this essay is potentially so diverse that it badly needs a logical plan to hold it together and avoid a narrative framework. The one suggested here compares the obvious causes with the deep-seated ones before showing how the reactions of the main participants made things worse.

Suggested essay plan *Introduction* Disputes over wages and hours seemed to be the main cause of industrial unrest, but there were also many underlying reasons.

1 Industrial unrest Police strikes in 1918 and 1919. Strikes of engineers and shipbuilders in Glasgow (for 40-hour week). One-week national rail strike against wage cuts. Coal miners threatened strike, but delayed until 1920: for wage increases and 6-hour day. 1921 three-month miners' strike against reduced wages. Threatened support from railwaymen and transport workers did not materialize. 1924: strikes of dockers (for 2 shillings a day extra), shipbuilders, etc. May 1926: miners locked out. Nine-day General Strike in support. Miners then held out for six months, before accepting longer hours and lower pay.

2 Underlying causes a) *Unstable prices* Most wages had not kept up with price rises during war. Inflation continued to 1920 and then prices fell by 30 per cent 1921–6.

b) *Post-war situation* War had upset economy. Coal mines and railways were run down and until 1921 were responsibility of the government. Huge national debt (interest over £325 million per year). Large-scale demobilization. European trade and industry recovered slowly.

c) *Industries in decline* Reduced world trade, increased foreign competition and new technologies led to serious decline for several leading nineteenth-century industries: coal mining, cotton, shipbuilding and some heavy engineering.

3 Reactions of main participants a) *Trade unions* greatly strengthened in war. Russian revolution encouraged trade union militancy and socialism. Bigger unions formed. 1919 alliance between miners, railwaymen and transport workers. From 1921 massive unemployment increased bitterness.

b) **Employers** reluctant to modernize their businesses. Used deflation as opportunity to cut wages. Often unsympathetic to employees: especially coal owners.

c) **Government** sympathetic to employers and frightened by Communist threat and economic problems. No real attempt to avoid confrontation. Teach workers harsh lesson. Non-interventionist. Ignored Sankey recommendation to nationalize mines. 1925 returned to Gold Standard: pound overvalued, exports suffered, especially coal. (Minority Labour government in 1924 not ready for power.)

Conclusion Huge gulf between organized workers and governing and employing classes in very difficult economic circumstances.

Chapter 7 *State Education in England and Wales to 1950*

Today the law forces all children to attend school for eleven of the most important years of their lives. It therefore seems natural that the state should raise huge sums of money from taxes to provide education for all 5 to 16 year-olds and to permit some older pupils to continue studying for several more years. However this is a comparatively recent development which began in a very small way about 150 years ago.

Schools 1780–1833

In the early nineteenth century schools were neither helped nor influenced by the government. They were run privately by individuals, societies or trustees. Parents decided if their children would attend and when they would leave. They usually had to pay.

Many upper-class children, especially girls, were educated at home by **tutors or governesses**, although the boys were also often sent to **large boarding schools** like Westminster, Eton and Rugby. Children from the professional and commercial middle classes attended a whole range of **academies and private schools**. These normally taught a wider curriculum than the classics of the **grammar schools** which were not popular.

Charity Schools
For the sons and daughters of the labouring poor there were some Charity schools. They taught reading and religion and possibly writing, arithmetic, shoe-making or needlework, especially in the larger villages and smaller towns. The rapid growth of population left the larger towns in particular short of schools. To help fill the gaps in town and country many individuals, including elderly women (**dames**), set up **schools in their own homes**. They rarely taught more than a little reading, knitting or sewing, but their charges were low and they kept the children out of mischief. There were also Sunday schools and monitorial schools.

Sunday Schools
These had developed nationally from 1780, inspired by **Robert Raikes** (1755–1811), a newspaper owner in Gloucester. Soon schools teaching only on Sundays were founded enthusiastically by Hannah More in Somerset, some factory owners and many Evangelicals and Methodists elsewhere. They welcomed the chance to try to get the rough and dirty children of the poor to read the Bible and respect their superiors. For tens of thousands of children this was their only chance of any education and in Wales many adults attended too.

Monitorial Schools
In 1798 **Joseph Lancaster** (1778–1838), a Quaker, opened a school for poor children

in London. In it he used older pupils or 'monitors' to instruct groups of younger children and then to test them with a rigidly structured series of questions. Often neither the monitors nor their pupils understood much of what they repeated, but by this system one teacher with very few books could supervise the teaching of hundreds of children. They learned to write on sand. Strict discipline was imposed with a system of rewards and punishments.

Because this monitorial method was so cheap, costing little more than five shillings a year for each child, Lancaster was soon supported by several wealthy backers including King George III. He founded the Royal Lancasterian Society in 1808 and a teacher training college at Borough Road, London, in 1809. But he was very difficult to work with, so that the society expelled him in 1814 and changed its name to the **British and Foreign Schools Society**, with strong support from the Nonconformist churches.

By then a rival society, the **National Society for the Education of the Poor**, had been founded in 1811 by **Andrew Bell** (1753–1832) to encourage the development of Church of England monitorial schools. Bell had developed a similar method of teaching in an orphanage at Madras in India, where he had been an army chaplain. He had described it in a book published in 1797, *An Experiment in Education*, and the supporters of the two men quarrelled over who had founded the monitorial system.

Intense religious rivalry between the British and National Societies led to keen competition to found new monitorial schools. Soon the National Society became far larger because of the greater wealth of the Church of England. Many existing village schools also took up the monitorial method. Robert Owen became one enthusiastic supporter. He was particularly interested in the education of infants and saw the need to have more teachers.

Together the British and National Societies increased the provision of education while the population was rising rapidly. This is shown by the fact that the proportion of brides and grooms who could sign their names when they got married had risen slightly by 1840 to about two-thirds of the men and half the women.

Government Support 1833–62

In 1833 the reforming Whig government decided to give some money to education for the first time. £20,000 was shared between the two societies for school building. The grant, which was renewed in the following years, rose to £30,000 by 1839, but the government had little influence over how it was spent. This was altered in **1839** when a **Committee of the Privy Council on Education** was set up. Its secretary was Dr James Kay (later **Kay-Shuttleworth**) (1804–77), who was a follower of Chadwick. Like many of his contemporaries, Kay-Shuttleworth believed that the children of the working classes would become more hard-working and better behaved when they grew up if they had a sound education first. In the 1840s Kay-Shuttleworth established the **Education Committee** as an effective means to help bring this about. (It was the forerunner of the Board of Education of 1899 and the Ministry of Education of 1944.)

Inspectors
The Education Committee appointed several inspectors (HMIs) to check that the

schools which received the grants were run efficiently. In the 1840s some £500,000 was given to the schools for furniture and apparatus as well as building. Four-fifths went to National Society schools because they raised most in voluntary contributions. The inspectors criticized increasingly the monitorial and Dame schools for being narrow and inefficient.

Teachers

Kay-Shuttleworth realized that more trained teachers were desperately needed, but because of religious opposition to state colleges only denominational training colleges were built.

To overcome the immediate shortage of teachers, Kay-Shuttleworth launched the **pupil-teacher system** in **1846**. Youths of 13 or 14 became apprentice teachers for five years. Each day they taught for 5½ hours under supervision and received 1½ hours instruction. If they passed an examination at the end they might become assistant teachers or win a Queen's Scholarship for a training college course. By the early 1850s there were some forty colleges in England and Wales with a total of 2,000 students, mostly from working-class homes. Pupil-teachers rapidly replaced monitors. There were 14,000 by 1861.

Other Developments

A range of other schools was developed at the same time for some of the poorest children. These included **workhouse schools** and part-time **factory schools** for young cotton workers following the Factory Acts of 1833 and 1844. **Ragged Schools** were also founded in towns from the early 1840s for the poorest vagrant children, who were often orphans. Lord Shaftesbury helped form the Ragged School Union in 1844. By 1870 the Union ran 132 ragged schools with 25,000 pupils, using voluntary funds.

Elementary Education for All 1862–99

In **1858** the **Newcastle Commission** was appointed to discover if there were better ways for the government to support elementary education for the working class. The grant paid to the efficient church schools had risen to £700,000 and those which needed help most did not get it. In 1861 the commission reported that most children received some education, but it was satisfactory for only about one-tenth. This was because few children attended long or regularly enough, and many teachers concentrated on their brighter pupils. To stop this and cut costs, the Newcastle Commission recommended that most of the schools' grants should depend on annual tests of each child by the inspectors.

Robert Lowe, the Vice-President of the Education Committee, introduced this **Payment by Results** system in the revised code of **1862**. Each child over the age of six could earn the school a grant of 4 shillings for good attendance and 8 shillings for passing the appropriate tests or standards in reading, writing and arithmetic. For a time the grant fell by £200,000 until the teachers learned to concentrate on the three basic subjects and make all pupils memorize their studies. Attempts to broaden their education with extra subjects had little effect until after 1882. The Payment by Results system was relaxed in 1890 and abandoned in 1898.

W. E. Forster's Education Act of 1870

The 1867 Reform Act, which gave the vote to many working men in the towns, helped convince the upper classes that they should be educated better. 'We must educate our future masters,' said Robert Lowe. In 1870 W. E. Forster's Education Act was passed to fill up the gaps left by the voluntary church schools. In areas where there were more children than school places, the ratepayers had to elect a **School Board** to provide new schools for 5 to 10 year-olds with money from both the rates and government grants. Parents were charged small weekly fees, fixed by each School Board, unless they were very poor. Attendance was not compulsory. The religious teaching could not be from any particular denomination (by the Temple-Cowper clause).

Because many people were more concerned with extending their own religious faith than in educating children, the voluntary societies made a huge effort to build more church schools. Their number rose from 8,800 in 1870 to 14,500 in 1900. By then there were 2,500 School Boards in England and Wales with 5,700 schools. However, most Board Schools were much larger because the biggest gaps had been in the largest towns and they were often better equipped. In 1895 nearly 2 million children attended them regularly and almost 2½ million the voluntary schools. Perhaps another 1½ million were absent all or most of the time.

Although School Boards were given the power in 1870 to enforce **attendance** on 5 to 13 year-olds, with exemptions from the age of 10, less than a quarter had done so by **1880**. Attendance was then made **compulsory** on these terms throughout the country. The age of exemption was raised to 11 in 1893 and 12 in 1899. An Act of **1891** made **elementary education free**. Compulsory attendance was difficult to enforce. It brought into the large town schools hordes of hungry children without shoes or proper clothes and suffering from infectious diseases. This underlined how bad living conditions still were in the towns.

The number of adult assistant teachers rose from 1,000 in 1870 to 28,000 in 1895 and there were even more pupil-teachers, but the classes were still huge, often with 80 or 90 pupils. In infant teaching a more child-centred approach was being developed, but for the older children the lessons remained dull and routine. And yet almost all children had learned to read and write by the end of the century. The proportion of people in England and Wales unable to sign their names at their weddings fell from 25 per cent of the men and 35 per cent of the women in 1861 to 3 per cent of both by 1901.

Secondary Education for All 1900–50

By the 1890s some Board Schools had formed special classes to teach more advanced subjects like science and French to their older and brighter children. In the large towns some School Boards even established separate Higher Grade Schools for those pupils who were likely to take skilled or clerical jobs in industry or business. However the 1870 Act allowed School Boards to spend rates only on elementary education.

In a test case that was engineered by Robert Morant in **1899, T. B. Cockerton** took the London School Board to court which ruled that these higher elementary classes were illegal. The voluntary societies were jealous of the success of the Board Schools. The grammar schools, which had been revived and reformed since the

Taunton Commission of 1864–8 and the Endowed Schools Act of 1869, also felt threatened. The administration of education had become chaotic with 2,500 School Boards, each voluntary and grammar school run separately and, since the Technical Instruction Act of 1889, the new County and Borough Councils responsible for giving grants and scholarships to secondary schools to encourage technical education. The Conservative government therefore seized the chance, deliberately created by the new Board of Education, to clear up this situation with a solution based on the Welsh Intermediate Education Act of 1889.

Balfour's Education Act of 1902
This abolished the School Boards and made the County and Borough Councils responsible for elementary and secondary education. These 318 new *Local Education Authorities* (LEAs) also had to maintain the buildings and pay the teachers in the voluntary schools despite bitter opposition from many Nonconformists. This greatly strengthened the church schools. Pupil-teachers soon disappeared and, as the number of adult elementary teachers increased (170,000 by 1920), women were very much in the majority. Teaching methods took longer to change.

The only other major development affecting elementary schools was the introduction of *welfare services* under the influence of Margaret McMillan. From 1906 the LEAs could provide school meals out of the rates. In 1907 they were forced to organize school medical examinations. Both measures helped improve the health of working-class children.

Grammar Schools
These gained most from Balfour's Act. It killed off higher elementary schools and gave the grammar schools financial help. Until 1919 they could receive a grant from the LEA and the Board of Education. After that they had to choose between one or the other. From 1907 those receiving a grant had to take at least a quarter of their pupils free from the elementary schools. Many new grammar schools were founded to supplement the existing ones.

By 1917 one-third of the grammar schools' 200,000 pupils held free places, which they normally gained by passing a test at about the age of eleven. With the ending of the pupil-teacher system, this was most working-class children's only chance of secondary education. The grammar school curriculum was designed for the requirements of university entrance and usually included little science or practical work. From 1917 grammar schools concentrated on preparing pupils for the new school certificate and higher certificate. Central schools with more vocational and less academic courses were developed in some towns from 1911. Their curricula underlined how limited most secondary education had become.

In *1918, Fisher's Education Act* raised the school-leaving age to 14. The Act's promises of nursery and continuation schools after 14 were killed by the depression of the 1920s and 1930s. Then the LEAs struggled to preserve the existing provision for education.

The numbers attending grammar schools continued to increase. By 1931 they had over 400,000 pupils, half of whom came in free. Then the parents of those who won a place were subjected to a means test, but by 1937 three-quarters of the grammar school pupils came from elementary schools. The grammar schools had been transformed.

Further Developments

In *1926, the Hadow Report* on *The Education of the Adolescent* recommended replacing this system with secondary education for all. Its suggestion for two stages of education, primary and secondary, with a break at about eleven, was taken up from 1928 mainly by urban authorities. They created senior departments and opened new senior or modern schools. By 1938 these contained two-thirds of all pupils over eleven. Most of the rest attended voluntary schools which were either unwilling or could not afford to reorganize.

The *Spens Report* on *Secondary Education* recommended in *1938* that children should be selected by intelligence tests, at the age of 11, for either grammar, modern or technical schools and eventually the school-leaving age should be raised to 16. The outbreak of war halted the plan to raise it to 15 in September 1939 and disrupted all education.

From 1942 *R. A. Butler*, the Conservative president of the Board of Education, planned for a better educational system after the war. His *Education Act* in *1944* accepted the Spens recommendations. Local authorities were required to provide secondary education free, according to the ability and aptitudes of the pupils. The raising of the school-leaving age was delayed from 1945 to 1947. The Board of Education was turned into a Ministry and the number of LEAs reduced to 146. These authorities were now required to provide school meals and free milk, regular medical inspection and special schools for eleven categories of handicapped children. All privately-run schools were to be inspected.

A new agreement was reached with the voluntary schools to help them cope with the costs of reorganization. They could choose between controlled or aided status, whereby the LEAs paid all or most of their expenses. In return all 'state' schools were required to give religious instruction and hold a daily act of collective worship.

Unlike the Act of 1918, the 1944 Education Act was implemented after the war. All pupils received free education up to the age of 15 and an increasing number continued after it. Of the 12–14 year-olds in 1951, over 5 per cent attended private schools, 2 per cent direct grant grammar schools and nearly 90 per cent 'state' schools. Within the LEA schools, 53 per cent attended modern schools, 16 per cent grammar schools and 3 per cent technical schools, while 14 per cent were still in all-age elementary schools.

Elementary education for all equipped children with certain basic skills needed for survival in the new industrial society. Secondary education for all unleashed a silent *social revolution*. Although some still had a privileged start, for most children their future jobs and social class would depend on their own educational qualifications more than on their parents.

Guide to Questions

Questions on education are usually set on the whole period covered by this chapter. Some will expect you to show detailed knowledge of particular Acts or developments, but many will also call for a wider understanding. Here are two examples of typical descriptive essays:

Write an account of elementary education during the nineteenth century. (Oxford, 1977). *What changes occurred in the provision and organization of state education between 1902 and 1951?* (Southern, 1979).

The structured essays and 'short notes' questions cover similar ground, but can be tackled with less careful planning:

What changes were made in the British educational system by the Education Acts of 1902, 1918 and 1944? (London, 1978). *Choose two of the following Education Acts. Explain the circumstances which brought them about, state their main terms, and suggest their chief results: 1870, 1902, 1944.* (Oxford, 1978). *Explain the significance of four of the following in the development of education: Sunday schools; Monitorial schools; Payment by results; School Boards; the 1902 Education Act; the Hadow Report, 1926; the 1944 Education Act.* (JMB, 1979).

Unlike many other topics, the examiners seem to set only straight-forward questions on education. With very few exceptions the essays in recent years have been descriptive and structured ones. 'Short notes' questions are normally the only kind of variety. Such questions should not pose any particular difficulties so long as you can remember the information accurately, appreciate the main points and write about them clearly.

Specimen Question 1

What were the main features of the education of the poor in England and Wales in the first half of the nineteenth century? (Oxford, 1978).

This is a descriptive question, which is asking you to describe the main ways in which the poor were educated between about 1800 and 1850. Your first problem will almost certainly be deciding who were the poor. Here the poor were not paupers who were helped by the Poor Law, but the great majority of the working classes or labouring poor as they were sometimes called. Labourers who earned little more than ten shillings a week could afford only to provide their families with basic necessities and so were poor. Otherwise this should not be a difficult question to plan, provided you do not stray off the point, by mentioning public schools, for instance.

Suggested essay plan **Introduction** In the early nineteenth century there were no state schools or compulsory education. The upper and wealthier middle classes normally paid to have their children educated. Most children of labourers started work as soon as they could and only had a few years schooling if it was free or very cheap.

*1 **Existing provision about 1800*** a) Charity schools. b) Sunday schools. c) Dame schools.

*2 **Monitorial schools*** a) Lancaster and British Society. b) Bell and National Society.

*3 **Government involvement*** (from 1833) Grants to societies. Education Committee (1839). HMIs. Pupil-teachers.

*4 **Other developments*** a) Factory schools: Acts of 1833 and 1844. b) Workhouse schools after 1834. c) Ragged schools from 1840s: very poor in towns.

Conclusion Provision of education more than kept pace with growth of population and poor. In 1850s Newcastle Commission discovered that most children attended school—at least briefly—but they were receiving a very inferior education.

Specimen Question 2

Explain why the Education Acts of 1870, 1902 and 1918 were important in the development of education in England and Wales. (Cambridge, 1978).

This is a structured question which might be answered most effectively in nine parts. To explain why each Act was important you will have to describe briefly the situation which it changed, its main terms and what it achieved. Obviously, you will have less to say about the 1918 Act than the other two, but still you must do it justice.

Suggested essay plan   *Introduction*   These three Acts played a crucial role in the growth of a national system of state education in England and Wales.

1 1870 Act   a) Importance of 1867 Reform Act. Limitations of voluntary schools, especially in the towns. b) Main terms of Forster's Act: elected School Boards to fill gaps and build and run schools. Undenominational religion. c) Compulsory education for all enforced eventually when enough schools existed. In 1870s by individual School Boards. 1880 Attendance compulsory (5 to 10 years old) but not free until 1891. By 1900 5,700 Board Schools and 14,500 voluntary schools (mostly smaller).

2 1902 Act   a) Voluntary schools short of funds. 1888 County Councils and Boroughs created. 1899 new Board of Education wanted to streamline educational administration. Cockerton judgement stopped School Boards spending money on higher grade elementary education. b) Main terms of Balfour's Act. 318 LEAs. Help for voluntary schools. Grammar schools brought under LEAs. c) Voluntary schools strengthened. Secondary school system developed rapidly with transfer to grammar schools at 11 by some elementary school children. Basis of system to 1944.

3 1918 Act   a) End of the war. b) Raised school-leaving age to 14 without exemptions. c) Promises of nursery schools and continuation schools for 14–16 year olds killed in 1920s by cuts in government spending.

Conclusion   1918 Act accepted principle of extending education beyond 5–14, but its failure showed that Acts of Parliament alone did not bring about educational change. It depended on a whole series of other developments as well.

Chapter 8 *Emancipation of Women 1870–1950*

Background to 1870

In the mid-nineteenth century Queen Victoria (1837–1901) and the vast majority of her subjects accepted without question the *traditional view of the family*. It was the basic unit of society, created by marriage which was a kind of business partnership. The partners had well-defined roles. The husband provided for, protected, ran and represented the family. The wife bore and reared children, fed and clothed the family and ran the house. Within the family, wife, children and any servants or lodgers were subordinated to its head, who owned all its property and supplied its name. Outside the family only the head mattered and unmarried adults had an inferior status to the married. The churches strongly supported this situation. Victorian Britain was clearly a man's world.

Middle-class Victorian Women
In the towns, women in prosperous middle-class families lived comfortably but depended entirely on their husband's occupation about which they knew little. Their behaviour was restricted by a strong social code, which prevented respectable ladies from working outside their homes and their daughters from having more than a superficial education.

Working-class Victorian Women
In most working-class households, low wages left the women struggling to keep their families fed, healthy and respectably turned out. Whenever possible they took the chance to earn a little extra money either in or outside their homes. Their daughters had equal opportunities with their sons for a few years of elementary education. Working-class girls often started work soon after the age of ten. Many became servants or worked in textile, clothing or other factories. Usually they did not marry until their later twenties, reared large families and died before their youngest child was grown up.

Changing Attitudes after 1870

After 1870 *the situation of women changed slowly* in many different ways both inside and outside their families, especially among the middle classes. The idea of marriage as companionship began to undermine absolute male domination. After the 1870s the *size of families began to decline* as women got married a little later and contraceptive practices began to be adopted. *Married Women's Property Acts* allowed wives to keep some of their earnings after 1870 and own their own property after 1882. Outside the family many more jobs developed in shops, post offices and offices, nursing and teaching that were considered suitable for respectable women.

The first Act for the prevention of cruelty to children was passed in 1889. The

Children Act of 1908 set up special juvenile courts and accepted the principle that the whole community was responsible for the treatment of young offenders. These, together with ***compulsory education*** and ***medical inspections***, began to ***undermine the absolute authority*** of working-class fathers in particular within their own families.

Educational Opportunities

By 1895 over a hundred new good-quality ***secondary day schools*** for middle-class girls were opened throughout the country, following the Endowed Schools Act (1869) and the creation of the Girls' Public Day Schools Company (later Trust) (1872). They were modelled on the North London Collegiate School (1850) of Frances Mary Buss (1827–94). Only a few girls' boarding schools imitated the Cheltenham College for Young Ladies where Dorothea Beale (1831–1906) had become principal in 1858. Soon after Balfour's Education Act (1902) girls were nearly as well provided with grammar schools as boys, and working-class girls were beginning to attend them.

Developments in ***higher education*** helped to gradually undermine further the widely held beliefs that women were born intellectually inferior to men. Thirty years after Queen's College, London, was founded in 1848 for training women teachers, London University allowed women to take degrees (1878). By then there were two women's colleges at Cambridge: Girton (which had moved from Hitchin under Emily Davies in 1873) and Newnham. At Oxford, Somerville College and Lady Margaret Hall were founded soon after. In 1876 Parliament allowed women to take exams set by medical schools, but Oxford and Cambridge did not permit their female students to take degrees like men for another forty years.

Votes for Women 1870–1945

The second and third Reform Acts (1867 and 1884) gave the vote in Parliamentary elections to many working-class men. This encouraged some women, and a few men like the philosopher John Stuart Mill, to campaign for the vote (or suffrage) for women.

Ever since 1834 all ratepayers (including some spinsters and widows) had been able to vote in elections for Poor Law Guardians. From 1870 female ratepayers could vote for and sit on School Boards, vote in County Council and Borough elections from 1888, serve on Boards of Guardians from 1894 and local councils from 1907. But still most MPs remained quite determined to keep women out of national politics. This finally convinced some women that the only way to achieve full emancipation (freedom) was to concentrate on winning the vote for Parliament and then use it to change many offensive man-made laws.

Organizations

The National Union of Women's Suffrage Societies was formed in 1897 to unite the many different organizations that had grown up in the previous thirty years to press for votes for women. Led by Mrs Millicent Fawcett, they were known as suffragists and tried to promote their cause by such means as threatening not to pay their taxes as well as by reasoned argument and legal propaganda.

In 1903 Mrs ***Emmeline Pankhurst*** (1858–1928) with her daughter Christabel founded a rival organization the **Women's Social and Political Union** (WSPU). Its members soon adopted much more militant tactics and were called **suffragettes**. The WSPU received strong support from the women textile workers in Lancashire, but their active members were mainly middle class. They soon included Mrs Pankhurst's second daughter, Sylvia. Mrs Pankhurst was the widow of a Manchester doctor. In the 1890s she had been an active socialist and campaigned for better conditions in the workhouses.

Suffragette Campaign

Although many MPs like Keir Hardie supported votes for women and Parliament discussed the issue several times during the next few years, it never passed an Act. In desperation the suffragettes resorted to tactics that became increasingly extreme. They started by heckling and interrupting the meetings of Winston Churchill, Lloyd George and other leading politicians. They organized impressive rallies and marches. They deliberately got themselves arrested and imprisoned: at first for minor offences, like chaining themselves to railings and scuffling with the police, and then for attacks on property, like breaking windows. In 1909 they started to go on hunger strike in prison and when some well-off and educated women were forcibly fed they won much sympathy.

The suffragettes also lost support by continuing to attack the Liberal government, which included many of their strongest allies. The suffragette campaign entered its last and most violent stage after the prime minister, Asquith, revealed in November 1911 that he favoured universal male suffrage to giving women the vote. Directed from Paris by Christabel, the WSPU became virtually an illegal organization, opposed by most of its former supporters. Even Sylvia finally split with her mother. These fanatical suffragettes attacked public buildings, paintings, golf courses and burned down houses. In 1913 Emily Davison was killed by the king's horse at the Derby.

Government Reaction

To cope with the hunger strikers Parliament passed 'the Cat and Mouse Act' in 1913. They could be released temporarily until they had recovered and then returned to prison to complete their sentence. Parliament could not now pass female suffrage without appearing to give in to intimidation. The First World War rescued both sides from this deadlock. The suffragette movement disintegrated as Emmeline and Christabel supported the government and encouraged the men to fight. Many women became nurses, while others joined the armed services, worked on the land and took up jobs, that had previously been reserved for men, in engineering and munitions factories or on the trams and buses.

The Right to Vote

Before the end of the war, the **Representation of the People Act** (June, 1918) gave the vote to all men over 21 and women over 30 who were householders or married to them. Out of 21 million voters, 8½ million were women. In 1928 the right to vote was given to all women over 21 on the same terms as men.

In 1918 women were also allowed to **sit in Parliament**. In December Christabel stood as a candidate in the general election and was defeated. The only woman returned was an Irish nationalist who refused to take her seat. In 1919 Lady Astor became the first female MP to enter Parliament. By 1929 there were 14, when

Margaret Bondfield became the first woman cabinet minister in the second Labour government. In 1945 the number of women MPs reached 24 out of 640. For many this was a very disappointing conclusion to the campaign for votes for women. However, Parliament did become more responsive to the pressure for more emancipation for women.

Further Emancipation 1919–50

Legal
In 1919 Parliament passed the *Sex Disqualification Removal Act*. This allowed women to hold all public offices, become JPs and enter the civil service, the universities and all professions except the church. In 1923 the *Matrimonial Causes Act* enabled a wife to sue for divorce on the same grounds as a man. In 1926 married and single women could hold and dispose of property on the same terms as men. In 1935 married women could dispose of all their property by will.

Social
Further steps towards emancipation were taken mostly by younger middle-class women. In the 1920s they started to smoke in public and go to cinemas and other places of entertainment without male escorts. They wore make-up and much lighter clothes in which they could move more freely. The work of pioneers in birth control, like Marie Stopes who opened a clinic in north London in 1921, at last made contraception within marriage respectable. But for at least another generation most young women knew little about how to prevent pregnancy and the sexual liberation of women remained very limited.

Employment
Many more jobs became available for women in the light engineering, electrical and chemical industries, but not in the depressed areas where working-class women suffered most severely from unemployment. In sharp contrast women in better-off homes gained most from rising standards of living and labour-saving devices like vacuum cleaners. During the Second World War women took up a wider range of jobs and in the 1940s all but a few ceased to be living-in domestic servants.

Full Equality?
By 1950 women had begun to marry earlier. With the continuing fall in the size of their families, the raising of the school-leaving age and the lengthening of life, most women were working for only a few years before marriage and for much longer after their youngest child had grown up. However, although great changes had been made in the family and in the way women lived, many barriers to full equality still existed, as the women's liberation movement showed clearly later. Most girls in 1950 still accepted without question that their main role in life would be as wife and mother.

Statistics

No. of children born	Changes in family size for marriages taking place in:		Declining family size for marriages in England & Wales at following dates which lasted 20 years or more:	
	England and Wales about 1860 (%)	Great Britain about 1925 (%)		
0	9	17	1860s	6.2
1–3	19	63	1870s	5.8
4–6	29	16	1880s	5.3
7–9	27	3	1890s	4.1
10 & over	16	1	1900s	3.3
			1910s	2.6
			1920s	2.2

Guide to Questions

Questions on this topic fall into two kinds. Those on the suffragettes tend to be more straightforward and easier to tackle. The only real catch in *Describe the aims, methods and achievements of the suffragettes.* (JMB, 1979) is in not overrating the influence of the suffragettes in securing votes for women, but this question does not ask you to discuss the other factors.

Questions on emancipation are generally much more wide-ranging. *In what ways did women become 'emancipated' between 1880 and 1951? Refer in your answer to: opportunities for education, property rights, occupations and rights to vote.* (Southern, 1976) is a much more helpful structured question than the following 'describe and explain' one: *For what reasons and by what stages have women obtained greater equality and freedom in the last hundred years?* (London, 1978).

Specimen Question
In what ways and for what reasons has the position of women changed since about 1850? (JMB, 1977).

This question is so wide and covers such a long period of time that deciding what to say and planning the essay will be equally difficult problems. Clearly you must not write a chronological account and it will not be easy to discuss adequately the position of both richer and poorer women. Also you must make sure that you give yourself enough time to explain why the position of women has changed as well as describing how it has happened.

Suggested essay plan   *Introduction*   Male domination of women in mid-Victorian family and society supported by laws and churches.

1 Changes within family   a) Birth control, smaller families, rising standards of living and improved health all helped position of women. b) State intervention and religious decline reduced power of male head of family.

2 Educational opportunity   Especially grammar schools and higher education. Women accepted as intellectual equals of men, but girls still not encouraged to take educational opportunities like boys.

3 Equality of treatment   a) Property owning and divorce. b) Right to vote: local & parliament. c) Employment: jobs, 1919 Act, later discrimination and equal pay. NB Upper and wealthy middle-class women tended to benefit first (and perhaps most) from many of these developments.

4 *Explanations* Great variety: a) Worldwide movement in developed countries, e.g. New Zealand women got the vote in 1893. b) Machinery increasingly reduced dependence on the physical strength of males. c) In war especially, the state needed to harness all its resources including woman power. d) In large towns large-scale social and economic change led to traditional roles of upper classes, men, etc. being questioned and then challenged. Movement for the rights of individuals won increasing support.

Conclusion Various campaigns led by articulate and able women who felt personally frustrated seemed very important at the time, but they were only a product of their times: A. Besant & M. Stopes (birth control), E. Davies (education), E. G. Anderson (medicine), E. Pankhurst (votes).

Chapter 9 *Economy and Society 1918–51*

This chapter will discuss three important topics from the first half of the twentieth century, all of which are interconnected: a) the main developments in British industry between the wars, b) unemployment and depression in the same period, and finally, c) the work of the Labour Government (1945–51).

Industry 1918–39

For two years after the First World War British industry prospered. The slump that followed was quite different from those before the war. Trade and industry did not revive after a few years but remained depressed for a long time, reaching a trough in the early 1930s before they began to revive. During this period different industries were affected very differently. Many of the old traditional industries declined or stagnated while some new industries emerged and even prospered.

Many causes contributed to this recession. During the later nineteenth century first the USA and Germany, and then Japan and other European countries, like France and Italy, had produced more and more manufactured goods. Because Britain's industries concentrated on supplying the armed forces during the war they lost many overseas markets to their foreign rivals and after the war they failed to win many back. Sometimes this was because these competitors had adopted more efficient machinery. Electricity was also beginning to challenge steam as a major source of power. Some British industry also suffered from a big drop in the prices of food and raw materials which left those countries which produced them unable to afford so many manufactured goods. Then in 1929 the Wall Street Crash, a catastrophic fall in the price of American shares, triggered off a massive slump which affected all Western countries in the early 1930s.

Old Industries
The cotton industry was hit hardest by the war. Before 1914 three-quarters of its output was exported. Because newly developing countries often turned first to cotton manufacture, Japan and India gradually ceased buying from Britain and became competitors instead. Most Lancashire cotton firms failed to install the latest machinery. Those producing coarser cloths suffered most. By 1933 Japan had captured the Far Eastern market and was already exporting more cotton goods than Britain. Cotton goods, which had formed 25 per cent of British exports in 1913, fell to 12 per cent by 1938. *Woollen textiles* fared much less badly because they had always relied much less on exports and concentrated more on high quality products.

The iron and steel industry experienced varying fortunes. During the war it had prospered mightily so that after the war there was a lot of surplus capacity. Most British furnaces were small and old-fashioned and their European rivals were better equipped to make 'basic' steel from phosphoric ores. During the early 1930s Britain's output of pig-iron and steel was halved, but then recovered after 1932 when imports were restricted by tariffs and quotas. Final recovery depended on rearmament before the Second World War. At the same time plants were modernized, larger firms created, great new steel works built at Corby, Scunthorpe, Ebbw Vale, etc., and the iron fields of the east Midlands developed until, by 1939, they produced three-fifths of British iron ore.

In 1910–14 British shipyards had built 60 per cent of the world's merchant shipping. Then the **shipbuilding industry** suffered very badly from the war when it could no longer meet many foreign orders and the USA in particular took over. After a brief post-war boom to replace the war losses, the demand for ships fell with the decline in world trade, but until 1929 Britain still launched over 40 per cent of the world's tonnage of new vessels. Disaster came with the great depression. By 1933 British yards launched only 7 per cent of their pre-war figure and in the next six years they did not fully recover. Most were older and smaller than their foreign rivals and not properly equipped to build the new type of motor vessels. By 1938 nearly one-third of the yards had been closed, some British owners had begun to buy ships from abroad and Germany was exporting more ships than Britain (who still launched one-third of the world's new tonnage).

During the 1920s the world's demand for *coal* ceased to expand rapidly because of the growing use of oil and electricity, the greater efficiency of steam-engines and the decline in world trade. British mines suffered from small collieries, narrow seams and out-dated machinery. After the Sankey Report (1919) recommending nationalization was rejected, they also suffered from bad labour relations and an inability to modernize in the face of greater output and efficiency in the European mines. Home demand levelled off at about 185 million tons a year and exports fell, as did prices. With more machinery (60 per cent of the coal was cut mechanically by 1939) fewer miners were needed. Their numbers fell from 1,200,000 in 1920 to 700,000 in 1938.

Newer Industries

In contrast to this gloomy picture a whole range of newer industries grew up and prospered at the same time. Most were light industries using electric power, and developed in the Midlands and the South-east, away from the coalfields. Their products included electrical equipment and goods like dynamos, electric motors, light bulbs, radios, cookers and vacuum cleaners, packaged and canned foods, aeroplanes and motor cars and chemicals.

Before 1914 the **motor-car industry** had developed on a small scale, mostly in the bicycle-making area of the West Midlands around Birmingham and Coventry. It concentrated on making, singly or in small batches, luxury cars for the rich. After the war it began to forge ahead by copying the American system of mass production based on standardized parts. **William Morris** (later Lord Nuffield) started making cars in Oxford in 1913 and was the British pioneer. In contrast to his predecessors Morris was an assembler rather than a manufacturer, who bought as many components as possible from their specialist makers. Sometimes he bought up the least efficient of his suppliers as well as other manufacturers, like Wolseley, to help him expand. By these methods Morris cut his prices and forced his rivals to adopt them too. In 1922 **Herbert Austin** introduced the Austin Seven, which became so popular that 350,000 were sold by 1938. Motor car output rose from 32,000 in 1920 to 182,000 in 1929, by when Morris and Austin made 60 per cent. Then the Americans entered the field in a big way, with Ford expanding at Dagenham and General Motors developing Vauxhall.

The response of most manufacturers to the great depression was to produce even cheaper and smaller cars, under 10 horsepower, in the early 1930s, like the Hillman Minx and the Morris Eight. With such intense competition output reached a peak in 1937 of 379,000 cars and 132,000 commercial vehicles. The number of car producing firms fell from 96 in 1922 to 20 by 1939, with six controlling 90 per cent of the market. Motor manufacture was now a major industry, with Britain producing the second largest number of vehicles in the world. The great majority was sold at home, where nearly 2 million cars and half a million goods vehicles were licensed for use on the roads by 1939. The growth of the motor industry encouraged many other industries including machine-tools, rubber and leather.

The **chemical industry** was one of the few new ones to be located partly in the depressed areas of Merseyside and the North-east. In 1926 four large firms merged to form **ICI** (Imperial Chemical Industries Ltd.) with a capital of £65 million. In 1932 it established international contacts. It had a wide range of interests covering dyestuffs, explosives, industrial gases, medicines, cosmetics, fertilizers and plastics. The chemical industry played an important part in the development of the first major man-made fibre, rayon, which was made from cellulose and cotton. In Britain its production was dominated by Courtaulds who established a factory at Coventry and also developed plastics and cellophane. But still Britain lagged far behind the USA, Germany and Japan and in 1939 the value of rayon exports was only one tenth that of cotton. Like most of the newer industries which developed in Britain it catered largely for the home market.

Statistics
The following figures show the extent of the post-war recovery of some industries and the later fluctuations in their fortunes.

	Industrial output (in million tons)			
	Coal (UK)	Pig-iron (GB)	Steel (UK)	Shipbuilding (UK) (ships commenced)
1913	287	10.3	7.7	1.9
1920	230	8.0	9.1	2.4
1928	238	6.6	8.5	1.3
1933	207	4.1	7.0	0.2
1938	227	6.8	10.4	0.5

NB Steel output was 5.3 million tons in 1932 and 13 million tons in 1937.

	Textiles (UK)				
	Raw cotton consumption	Lancashire cotton factories		Numbers employed	
		Spindles	Looms	in cotton	in wool
	(million lbs)	(millions)	(thousands)	(thousands)	
1913	2,200	59	785		
1920	1,700	60	800 *(1923)* 570	270	
1928	1,500	60	755	555	245
1933	1,200	54	600	500	230
1938	1,100	41	460	395	215

	Houses built (GB) (thousands)	Cars and commercial vehicles built (UK) (thousands)	Electricity generated (UK) (million kWh)	Numbers employed in coal industry (UK) (millions)
1913	54	34	1,300	1.13
1920	30	*(1922)* 73	*(1920)* 4,300	1.25
1928	205	210	9,400	0.94
1933	275	285	13,700	0.79
1938	360	445	24,600	0.79

Unemployment in 1920s and 1930s

In the sixty years before the war one worker in twenty had been fully unemployed on average, and at the worst moments the proportion rarely rose above one in ten. This pattern continued in the two years after the war even though at the same time three million soldiers and sailors returned to civilian employment.

All this changed in 1921 when the percentage unemployed rose to 15 with a peak of 22 per cent from April to June during the coal stoppage. Employment improved in 1924 and again in 1927–9, but still the official unemployment rate did not fall below 10 per cent. Then it rose to over 20 per cent for nearly three years in the great depression of the early 1930s, reaching a peak of 23 per cent in August 1932. After 1933 things improved until one in ten was unemployed in 1937, but then, even with rearmament, it worsened slightly in 1938–9. These official figures applied only to those workers who were covered by the Insurance Acts. Agricultural workers, domestic servants, civil servants, police, railwaymen and the self-employed were among those excluded and in the worst years others did not bother to register. The official totals of unemployed can therefore be misleading. In 1931 the true total of unemployed must have been about 3.3 million rather than 2.7 million and at its peak in 1932 around 3.75 million. When their close families are included this means that at least 6.7 million were living on the dole in the early 1930s.

General unemployment percentages hide very great differences between industries, areas and workers of different skills, ages or sex. Before 1914 London and the South had been affected worst. In the 1920s the traditional northern industries which relied most on exports suffered worst: coal mining, cotton, iron and steel, and pottery. Almost no industry escaped the effects of the world economic depression from 1929. During the ensuing recovery many workers moved into the expanding industries from the declining ones.

In selected industries	Unemployment percentages		By regions (average 1929–36)	
	1932	1937		
Shipbuilding	62	24	South-west	8
Pig-iron making	43	10	London	9
Coal mining	34	15	South-east	11
Cotton	28	11	Midlands	15
Wool and worsted	21	10	North-west	22
Motor vehicles	20	5	Scotland	22
Food industries	17	12	North-east	23
Electrical engineering	16	3	Wales	30

Within each industry the unskilled workers bore the brunt of unemployment. In 1931, for instance, 30 per cent of the unskilled labourers were unemployed compared with 14 per cent of the skilled and semi-skilled industrial workers and 6 per cent of the white collar workers. Long-term unemployment (12 months or more) also varied between the regions. In 1936 they formed 37 per cent of the unemployed in Wales and 9 per cent in London and the South-east. And within the regions unemployment was much more severe in particular towns. In 1934, for instance, the percentage in Jarrow was 68, Merthyr Tydfil 62 and Gateshead 44. There were also special problem groups like many boys and girls who were shunted into dead-end jobs on leaving school and then made unemployed when they became old enough to claim full wages. The misery, bitterness, poverty, demoralization and hunger caused by unemployment could be found anywhere, but clearly it was concentrated in the older industries on and near the coalfield.

Government Action
Before the war the Liberal government had passed two measures to help the unemployed. From **1910 Labour Exchanges** helped inform them about vacant jobs. The **National Insurance Act (1911)** covered all manual workers for sickness, but for unemployment only about three million in trades like shipbuilding, building and iron-founding. In return for a small weekly contribution they became eligible when unemployed for 7 shillings a week for a maximum of 15 weeks in any one year. In 1920 unemployment insurance was extended to about another 8 million: everyone earning less than £5 a week except for farm labourers, domestic and civil servants and some others. The weekly benefits were raised to 15 shillings for men and 12 shillings for women.

Clearly this system was not designed to cope with prolonged unemployment, but only to tide people over while they looked for another job. In 1921 therefore the government introduced allowances of 5 shillings for a wife and 1 shilling for each dependent child, and extended benefits, nicknamed **the dole**, for those still unemployed after 26 weeks. But there was even a time limit to the dole so that when it was finished poor relief became the last resort. The scales paid varied from place to place. In the London borough of Poplar and some other Labour-controlled areas, the Guardians paid rates well above those approved by the Ministry of Health. Their opponents therefore described the 'squandering of other peoples' money' on the unemployed as 'Poplarism'. The Poplar councillors also claimed that the high cost of poor relief prevented them from paying their share of London County Council expenses. They were imprisoned in 1921 for their defiance.

A committee of businessmen, set up by the government to advise it on how to cope with the slump, reported in 1922. Led by Sir Eric Geddes, they advocated cutting taxes and public expenditure, including education, health, unemployment benefits and the civil service as well as the army and navy. The government did not accept all their recommendations, but when they did wield the **'Geddes axe'** education was devastated most. This set the tone for all governments up to 1939 to respond to economic difficulties by attacking the poor and economically weak.

The biggest cuts were made in 1931 when the minority Labour government which could no longer control the economy, was replaced by a National government consisting mainly of Conservatives and Liberals. Although it cut the pay of all public employees by 10 per cent it could not prevent the pound from losing a quarter of its value by leaving the Gold Standard, to which it had returned only six years earlier in 1925. Unemployment benefit was not only cut by 10 per cent but more money was saved with the 'means test'. After his 26 weeks of benefit ran out an unemployed man's relief now depended on the total income of all members of his household, which could be very humiliating for him. From 1932 the government tried to protect British industry with import duties, but even though concessions were made to imperial countries, it had little effect except to restrict world trade further.

Usually the unemployed suffered in silence. Occasionally public demonstrations drew attention to their plight. In 1936 200 men marched from Jarrow, in Durham, to London to protest at the dismantling of their shipyard. They aroused sympathy but no effective action. Only World War II banished unemployement.

Labour Government 1945–51

Attlee's was the first majority Labour government. It won a huge overall majority of 147 in the election of July 1945, and stayed in power from 1950 with a tiny majority of 6. Clearly the British people voted in 1945 for social and economic change, hoping to avoid the miseries of the inter-war depression.

A mammoth task faced the new government. Britain was almost bankrupt and many towns had been devastated by bombs. Food, clothes and fuel which had been very short during the war became even more scarce immediately after it, while Europe and parts of the rest of the world needed urgent resettlement. However, the government was not toally inexperienced. Among the new Cabinet ministers only Aneurin Bevan (1897–1960), the Minister of Health, had not held office in Churchill's wartime coalition. Clement Attlee (1883–1967), the Prime Minister, had been deputy Prime Minister, Herbert Morrison (1888–1965), Attlee's deputy, had been Home Secretary, Ernest Bevin (1881–1951), Foreign Secretary, had been Minister of Labour and the successive Chancellors of the Exchequer, Hugh Dalton in 1945–7 and Sir Stafford Cripps in 1947–50, had also held important posts under Churchill.

Welfare State

During the war some ministers had been concerned with reconstruction after it. In 1942 a committee under Sir William Beveridge, a senior civil servant, had devised a plan to provide social insurance for everyone by co-ordinating and improving the existing schemes. The *Beveridge Report* proposed that in return for one single weekly contribution all citizens should receive benefits, without a means test, when they were sick, unemployed, retired or widowed, to allow them to maintain a certain minimum standard of living. He also recommended paying weekly family allowances to parents for each dependent child. This report, which was welcomed more warmly by the Labour ministers than the Conservatives, was the biggest single influence on the forming of the Welfare State.

Family Allowances were the first to be introduced. From August 1946 five shillings a week was paid for each child after the first up to the age of sixteen or the start of full-time employment, if that was earlier. By the *Industrial Injuries Act* (1946) the Ministry of National Insurance which had been set up in 1944, became responsible for paying compensation to all who were injured, disabled or killed at work, and additional supplements to their dependants. Then the *National Insurance Act* (1946) implemented the main proposals of the Beveridge Report from July 1948. Everyone of working age, except married women, had to pay weekly contributions and, when appropriate, they became entitled to sickness, unemployment and maternity benefits, retirement and widows' pensions, guardians' allowances and a funeral grant. At first employed persons paid 4s 11d a week, for example, while the unemployed and the retired both received 26 shillings weekly. Finally in 1948 *National Assistance Boards* were established to cater for those who were not covered by insurance or whose needs could not be met fully, like the blind, crippled, deaf, insane, homeless, deserted or unmarried mothers and some elderly people. National Assistance payments were means tested.

The *National Health Service Act* (1946) improved on the coalition government's plans for a free state medical service. Everyone was covered and not just wage-earners as previously. The NHS provided general practitioner, hospital, specialist, ambulance, dental, midwifery and child welfare services together with drugs, medicines, spectacles and dentures. Almost all were totally free and financed mainly out of taxation. This scheme came into effect on 5 July 1948 along with National Insurance and National Assistance. Because it was opposed so bitterly by many doctors through the British Medical Association, Bevan was forced to make some concessions. Most teaching hospitals, medical and dental schools were not brought under the Ministry of Health, the hospitals could have beds or wards for private patients and doctors were normally paid fees and not salaries. Because the cost of the health service soon soared much higher than anticipated, part of the cost of dental treatment and spectacles was charged to the patient in 1951 and Bevan, who was then Minister of Labour, resigned from the government in protest.

Re-housing and the re-planning of cities had a high priority in the plans for post-war reconstruction. But high costs and a shortage of materials and skilled tradesmen led to half the number of houses being built per year (170,000) compared with 1934–9 (358,000). Even though the vast majority were council houses, a chronic housing shortage remained. Under the *New Towns Act* of 1946 fourteen new towns were established, eight of them near London (Stevenage, Crawley, Bracknell, etc.), but they were not fully developed until the 1950s.

Nationalized Industries
During the war the government controlled almost every aspect of national life, including industry and agriculture. In peacetime the Labour Party believed in preserving much state control because it seemed a more efficient way of managing scarce resources and because it did not believe that necessities like fuel, power and transport services should be run for private profit. Between 1946 and 1949 the Labour Government therefore put through a large programme of nationalization.

In 1946 the *Bank of England* was nationalized. So were the coal mines, which in 1947 were placed under the *National Coal Board* which began a vast modernization scheme. *Civil Aviation* was brought into public ownership at the same time: originally under three airways corporations which were reduced to two in 1949 (BEA and BOAC). The *Public Transport Act* (1947) came into effect in 1948 with six executive boards under the British Transport Commission administering the Railways, (BR), London Transport, (long-distance) Road Haulage, (BRS), (some) Road Passenger Transport, Docks and Inland Waterways and Hotels. By the *Electricity Act* (1947) the generation, supply and distribution of electricity came under the British Electricity Authority with twelve area boards in place of the Central Electricity Board. Similarly the *Gas Act* (1948) created a nationalized Gas Council with twelve area gas boards. Lastly, an Act of 1949 set up in 1951 the short-lived *Iron and Steel Corporation*, which (like road haulage) was denationalized by the Conservatives in 1953.

Although these measures gave the government considerable control over large areas of the economy, they were not opposed strongly by the Conservatives, except for iron and steel. There the firms were relatively efficient and profitable, but in most of the other industries the private owners put up little resistance because they were unable to finance the extensive improvements that were needed, especially in the mines and railways, caused by years of neglect both before and during the war. After paying substantial compensation to the owners and share-holders (£165 million to the coal owners for instance) the government also had insufficient resources. And so the public noticed comparatively little difference after nation-alization and soon started to complain about inadequate services. Alienation from the nationalized industries was accentuated by the form in which they were organized. Herbert Morrison insisted that they should be managed by public corporations, whose members were appointed by the minister responsible, but neither he, nor the workers, nor the users could interfere in the daily running of these boards. Thus the management was protected from persistent and ignorant interference so long as they made a profit (which most did not), but this did not develop a sense of public service.

By nationalizing these industries and developing the Welfare State the Labour government implemented its promise to create a more socialist state and, after 1951, the Conservatives accepted that this was largely what the people wanted.

Guide to Questions

The questions are usually divided into three topics: industry 1918–39; unemploy-ment; and the Labour government 1945–51. The majority of the industry questions deal with the problems of the traditional heavy industries, or with the growth of new ones, like motor cars, electrical goods, etc., with, occasionally, both old and new industries linked in one question, e.g. *Each of the sections below lists two British industries. Choose one section and describe and contrast the development (1918–39) of the two industries listed in the section: a) shipbuilding: motor car manufacture; b) cotton cloth manufacture: electrical goods; c) coal mining: house building.* (Southern, 1977). You are expected to know why the old industries contracted, and how far the problem had been solved by 1939. The vast majority of these questions are 'describe and explain', as they are with the causes of the depression in the 1930s, and with unemployment. In both cases, you are asked about government action, and, sometimes, particular areas, e.g. *Explain why unemployment in the 1930s was so high in Lancashire, South Wales and the North-east, but low in the Midlands and the South-east of England. What did the government do to help the depressed areas?* (JMB, 1979).

Most questions on the Labour government 1945–51 deal with nationalization or the Welfare State. Some general questions are asked, on the general problems this government faced, with the occasional 'imagine' question, e.g. *What economic problems did the Labour government have to face in the years 1945–50, and how did it tackle these problems?* (Oxford, 1977), and *Imagine that you are a Labour Member of Parliament elected in 1945. Outline the measures affecting economic and social life which your party intend to introduce.* (London, 1980). Sometimes, the Beveridge Report is referred to, and you are certainly expected to know its contents thoroughly.

Specimen Question 1
The years 1918–39 brought serious difficulties to heavy industry (coal, iron and steel, shipbuilding) in Britain. What circumstances caused these difficulties and how effectively had they been overcome by 1939? (Oxford, 1979).

This is an 'explain' question, asking you to deal with the reasons for the problems faced by heavy industry and whether they had found solutions by 1939. You need to set a context for the question, since these industries were not the only ones to meet problems: the 1920s and 1930s was a difficult economic period internationally, and you should show that you know that. The three industries did vary in their problems and the ways they reacted to them, but there were a number of common reasons for their problems and these need to be emphasized. The key word in the last part of the question is 'effectively': none of these industries had solved their problems 'effectively' by 1939.

Suggested essay plan *Introduction* Initial prosperity after 1918: then long depression into 1930s; different industries affected in different ways.

1 *General* British industry on defensive since late nineteenth century: heavy industry especially. Production 1914–18 based on war effort: machinery out of date by 1918. Loss of overseas markets. Effect of Wall Street Crash, 1929.

2 *Coal* Increased use of oil and electricity: decline in world demand for coal. British mining inefficient; poor labour relations: culminating in General Strike, 1926. Modernization would involve closing smaller mines, unemployment, and great capital investment. More machinery was used: by 1939 60 per cent of coal cut in that way, but also fall in numbers of miners.

3 *Iron and Steel* Had done well 1914–18. But furnaces old-fashioned: rivals better equipped: considerable decline in British output. After 1932: improvement, since government introduced protective tariffs. Some modernization, new steel works, and east Midlands fields were developed.

4 *Shipbuilding* Short prosperity after 1918; then, decline in world trade: decline in demand for shipping. Britain did reasonably well until 1929: by 1933 British yards launched 7 per cent of 1914 figure. Yards old, not well equipped to produce new types of ships. By 1938, about one-third of yards closed, owners buying ships abroad. Britain still launching a third of world's new tonnage, but Germany exporting more ships.

Conclusion These industries varied in their difficulties, but all suffered from out-of-date equipment and foreign competition. Revived by the outbreak of war in 1939.

Specimen Question 2

Why was unemployment so serious a problem in Britain between the two World Wars? What measures did governments adopt to solve it, and how successful were they? (Oxford, 1976)

This is a structured 'describe and explain' question. The first part of the question demands the explanation and the description deals with government policies, and then whether they were successful or not. It is probably easier to deal with these points altogether, rather than to divide your answer into three separate parts.

It is necessary to explain the general problem between 1921, when unemployment began to get worse, and 1939, and it is best to do this first, since it deals with the first part of the question. This needs to be followed by an explanation of the regional variations in unemployment, and you can include some of the statistical information from the chapter, but not necessarily in table form. If you look at the figures, you should be able to draw some conclusions from them. Government action and its effect needs to be set against all government attempts to cut back on spending as one way of trying to control the economy.

Suggested essay plan *Introduction* 1918–20 unemployment similar to before

1914. After 1921 it reached previously unknown levels; not temporary, nor dependent on trade cycle.

1 General problem Include information on the 1920s and 1930s, showing how unemployment varied, e.g. 22 per cent in 1921; very high in early 1930s; 10 per cent by 1937. Point out that these are minimum figures: they do not include workers not included by the Insurance Acts.

2 Decline of traditional industries 1920s: old industries suffered most. 1930s: some migration of workers to more prosperous areas. Unskilled workers affected most. Include some detailed information from the chapter in this paragraph.

3 Government action a) Pre-War National Insurance Act not designed to cope with this type of unemployment. 1921: 'the dole'; yet 'Geddes axe' began government cut-backs lasting to 1939; biggest cuts 1931. Introduction of means test. b) Some government action positively harmful, e.g. return to the Gold Standard in 1925. c) return to Protection in 1932. Therefore, government action limited in scope and effectiveness. Problem only really solved by outbreak of war in 1939.

Conclusion Unemployment vast and continuous in 1920s and 1930s. Governments unable to find solution. Cuts in government spending affected benefits paid. Very little direct help for industry.

Specimen Question 3
In what ways did the Labour government of 1945–50 develop the Welfare State? (Southern, 1977)

In spite of its wording, using the phrase 'in what ways', this question is a descriptive one, and should read *Describe how the Labour government of 1945–50 developed the Welfare State*. As such, it is reasonably straightforward, requiring a description of the three main stages: those in 1946; the National Insurance Act, 1948; and the setting up of the National Health Service in 1948. A section is needed at the start of the essay to explain that the Beveridge Report of 1942 was a great influence upon the Labour Party, although you should also point out that many Labour supporters believed that these welfare reforms reflected their socialist beliefs.

Suggested essay plan *Introduction* First majority Labour government under PM Attlee. Elected on a programme of economic and social change.

1 Beveridge Report Committee set up in 1942. Include details of its contents, especially about the sick, old, and unemployed. Report had great impact upon Labour ministers and great influence upon establishment of Welfare State.

2 First stages 1946: family allowances; also the Industrial Injuries Act. Include the main points of both of these.

3 National Insurance Act 1946 To operate from July 1948. Weekly contributions, widespread benefits. e.g. unemployment and sickness payments, widows pensions, etc., 1948: National Assistance Boards: for those not covered by the 1946 Act: give examples, and point out that payments were means tested.

4 National Health Service 1948 National Health Service Act. Provided free medical service as a right. Specialist care paid out of taxation. Problems faced by Aneurin Bevan. Cost high: extra charges in 1951 and Bevan resigned.

Conclusion These measures were the product of war and of the Labour Party's commitment to a more socialist state. The Conservative Party continued the Welfare State after 1951. It accepted that it was what people wanted.